If there was one thing that you could say that you know beyond anything, beyond refute, without imagining, without speculating, what would that be?

Averi
and the
UNKNOWN

'FROM THE LIGHT OF WISDOM'

Awakening to the Heart of Love

SARASWATHI MA

BALBOA
PRESS
A DIVISION OF HAY HOUSE

Balboa Press books may be ordered through booksellers or by contacting:

Balboa Press
A Division of Hay House
1663 Liberty Drive
Bloomington, IN 47403
www.balboapress.com
1 (877) 407-4847

ISBN: 978-1-4525-4335-2 (sc)
ISBN: 978-1-4525-4336-9 (e)

Library of Congress Control Number: 2011961618

Printed in the United States of America.

Balboa Press rev. date: 8/25/2014

ACKNOWLEDGEMENTS

My sincere gratitude to Valerie, Sallyanne, Victor, Sacha, Victorio, Graham, Martin, Maria, Zenji, Garry and Margrethe, for reading and expressing, and for bringing me back to my Self.

With special thanks to Rita, for sifting through with precision and patience.

My love to Gaia for guiding, to Francesca for framing, and to Dwight for directing the way.

And, finally, my love and gratitude to Valerie, Ann, Paul and Sebastien for making it possible.

Thank you.

For, through and by the Grace of
Sri Sathya Sai Baba

For beloved Mooji, for bringing my mind to my Heart

For LJR; my twin, my light, my teacher

Words have cradled
to caress without effort.
I love That.

I am stoked,
Ablaze;
Finely enunciated,
Sung with Grace.

Sweet words, know Me.
I am all out of which this voice was born.
Blessed cantata;
I *am* That.

PART ONE

1

⚔

One evening a being named Averi[1] was chopping vegetables in the kitchen of his wooden home. The carrots were already done, cut into wide rings instead of sticks, for these were the makings of a fine stew. Averi put down his knife and picked up the peeler. Inside came a twinge of impatience, for although he enjoyed swede very much indeed, it always appeared as slightly more effortful to prepare than the other vegetables. Averi stopped. Along with that twinge had come a thought, or at least it appeared as a thought. But it had raced so silently across the screen of his vision that he had absolutely no idea what the thought had been. Averi rested the heels of both hands on the chopping board and stared down at the grain of the wood, at the red of the pepper, at the mottled green of the courgette.

---

1   Averi – pronounced: *ah-very*

A thought had come, it had been too fast to register, but Averi had seen it nonetheless.

At that moment a ladybird skirted the circumference of his knuckles. It seemed to be making a clear line towards the ring of the electric hob where the onions were frying in a pan. Averi's eyes followed this determined friend. A thought came to turn off the hob, but Averi had come to such a standstill that all movement seemed impossible. Nevertheless, he watched his arm lift up and reach across to the dial. He saw his fingers turn the temperature to zero and draw the pan towards the ladybird, so as to prevent the little fellow from reaching the rim of cooking heat. Averi watched all this as if his arm and fingers were quite independent of him. And then the most unusual thing occurred. Averi realised that he had *watched* the thought to turn off the hob when it came, just as he had *seen* the thought that had been too quick to decipher. Averi blinked hard. His eyes had begun to smart from the sweat of the onions, and so he stepped away from the stove and the chopping board, crossed the wooden floor of his wooden kitchen and opened the kitchen door onto sharp October air that frisked his nostrils and his ear ways. There were gulls in his hearing and the slick tang of sea salt on his tongue. Could it have been his dream last night that was causing this confusion? Certainly, it had played on his mind all day, for not a word of it made any sense. Averi breathed, slowly and deeply, consoled by the brush of high tide.

The next morning held a grey sky. It hung low on the rooftops of all the wooden houses, deep-pitted and heavy jowled. Rain had come to stream-line the town and Averi was glad of it. It was running still in rivulets and the smell licked his pores. A wind, too, was in the air; not quite arrived, but warning. The great firs at the side of the road were shifting uneasily. Averi stopped at the bottom of the hill and listened. A north-easterly, for certain; but its smell was unusual. If he was very still, Averi could discern the best course for a catch. But this blow was foreign, a scent with secrets he could not yet decipher. He was unnerved at not knowing; the boys would ask and he would have no answer to give them. Averi kept to the walk. It was alarming to find himself anxious, and this early morning climb would brace him.

It was certainly the best the town had to offer. The road rose, ever so steeply, up and away from the shore, past more wooden houses – for many houses were wooden in the days to come, and it was a rare thing indeed to see a dwelling of stone or the red brick of Pisces as folk were apt to call it – until it reached the centre of Quartermaine itself. There, on the corner opposite the hardware store, was the Boat Shop. Averi tucked his chin into the neck of his wind-breaker and crossed to the window to look. A giant lobster pot hung down from a chain and clustered around it were all the things that Nyx liked to sell. The fishermen of Quartermaine always came here: he and Trindar, Raul, Haiti and Patch. Nyx sold them their wind-breakers, their bibs, their braces, their sou'westers and their great yellow boots. But anyone with a taste for tackle or fishing-rods might find here what they were looking for: perhaps books on tides, on navigation, on the hundreds of species that Averi had never even seen come into the warehouse; on dolphins and seals and turtles from the Exotics, and the mythical whale-fish; and boxes of bait if you didn't mind putting your hand in and collecting a pound-full

yourself. This was Nyx's special joke. Today, she was
there already, earlier than all the other shop-holders,
standing behind the counter with her head bowed low
over a ledger. Her hair hung free, dark and smooth as
the tone of her skin. Averi lowered his eyes and turned
away. If he was late the boys would know why.

The warehouse sat squat and blue-boarded on the
harbour wall. Years of salt had seeped into the grain,
whitening and wrinkling the paintwork. That was why
Averi and the boys called her the Old Lady. She was
weatherworn and faded and all the more beautiful for it.
Averi took off his glove and felt the wood of the window
frame. When the weather was drier this would need
stripping and sanding. Weatherworn was one thing,
rotten was another.

Herring gulls, the morning party, were tussling for
breakfast. Averi turned to watch and, as he turned, what
he saw was *panoramic*. He froze. Here it was again, the very
same that had come before the stew last night. The very
same that had left the stew uncooked and unimportant.
The very same that had sat him most of the night on
the decking, unable to move despite the cold eating his
bones: the strangest feeling that had swallowed him
whole until nothing existed but space. In front of him, it
was not the view itself that was panoramic. This was as
it always was: the concave of the land like a giant crab's
claw, the harbour – a man-made pouch that held just
enough for two dozen boats, and the great ocean a little
greyer than usual and frothy in patches where the wind
was hustling. But what was *experienced* was panoramic
in a way that Averi knew and yet did not know. Fresh
as an old friend it seemed. Inward and yet outward. It

was neither one nor the other, but so broad as to have no edges. The gulls continued, oblivious, their raucous cries heard in a silence without end. *Chariot* was there, rocking as if impatient, her scrubbed deck glistening still from the rain. A red woollen hat peered out of the hold. It was Trindar, his unfeasible bulk a comfort. He waved. Averi felt his arm wave back as if it were no longer attached to him. An arm that did as it was bade to do, except that he had not even bid it. He was smiling, too, that he was certain of; a smile that reached into the back of him and went beyond.

- Quite a blow it's kicking up, Skip.

It was Haiti taking him by surprise, with his deep voice and a one-armed hug. Haiti loved a squall, and the light of a rough sail shone in his eyes.

- It's a blow, alright, Averi replied. Yeah.

The warehouse doors swung back on their hinges and there was Patch, so swaddled you could barely make out the shape of him. Patch believed in layers, perhaps because there was so little of him. Roll necks and sweaters and great padded waterproofs and a brown woollen balaclava under his hood. There was no sign of his namesake, the patch of white hair in brown. What a collection of days it had been since the other children had first pointed their fingers. Averi had knelt down, that school day morning, to retrieve the carved sailing boat that had been kicked like a sport-ball across the yard. The rudder had been badly scraped and the top sail had flapped weakly like a broken wing. Patch had smiled his first smile at Averi, a little like now, unafraid and quizzical.

Averi felt his legs move beneath him. How light and agile and soft came his step, moving within this panorama. His senses were there in front of him.

Listening was happening, that was certain. Sounds were moving as if across a wide vista. If he chose to, he could pinpoint one and tune in as if it were a radiogram. Then, quite as suddenly, once interest was lost, listening occurred again without distinction. Seeing was happening too, seeing in a wide expanse. It took in the clutter of the warehouse and the gillnets and the double fykenets, the weights and the floats, and the upside-down rowing boat they had still not stripped; the lobster pots piled in the corner, Haiti's bicycle with its year-old puncture, shackles, thimbles, grips and swivels, and the little black stove in the middle. Averi held out his hand to steady himself. He found the tin drum and sat down upon it. And now here came smell. Patch had crossed to the stove where he was boiling milk in a pan. The ritual was as it always was: black leaves soaked until strong, then strained through a sieve into blue enamel mugs with several spoons of brown sugar and boiling hot milk. One mug was then poured from a height into another mug, so that the tea might be properly mixed. It was a time-consuming process, perhaps three or four pourings back and forth for each mug. This was Patch's way, and no one argued for the tea tasted fine.

Averi blinked hard. If seeing and listening and smelling were happening within him then, came the question – bright as Sirius – what *knew* this? It may have been an answer that came, but even if it was Averi had not the words to express it. All he knew was that everything dropped away. As if he had been turned inside out and his organs had melted into space.

~ Like hell we'll make it out the bay. It's a frighted easterly, alright, an' we ain't no match fer it.

Raul threw off his oilskin as he entered the warehouse. It was his way of a challenge to the wind. Straight to the stove he walked and to the first prepared mug. Raul did not wait for civilities, or for the tea to cool. He drank it, burning milk and all.

- You ever sin it so raging?

Averi saw that the question was aimed at him. But Raul rarely wanted an answer. He preferred to snort his own into the echo of his cup.

Averi made the move across to the stove and picked up his tea. Patch and he seldom spoke in the mornings, but today Patch looked at him squarely, his quizzical eyes raised and his mouth open. No words came, though, none verbal at least. Averi wondered if he had guessed about his dream and that he, Patch, his closest friend, was at the centre of it. But that was ridiculous. How could Patch know about his dream? For a moment, Averi wished that he did, that they were alone and able to talk about it. But this, too, was ridiculous. He could barely even describe it to himself. Averi looked away and drank, grateful for the heat and for Raul's bluster. Haiti's arm was again upon his shoulder and Trindar's heavy step and wheeze were following behind. They stood all five around the heat of the stove as the easterly worked itself up. Haiti had a theory that if you ignored a strong wind, its fury would soon dispel like a child who has lost all attention. But today it was adamant. The warehouse door slammed shut and a great sigh swept around the hut as if it were lashing it tight. Raul looked up, cross and fearful; Trindar wheezed, unperturbed; Patch had both ears on alert, his blue eyes hungry with wonder; and Haiti began to sing, his deep baritone of a lullaby broad, fathomless, coaxing. Averi looked to his friends – his own ears tingling with certainty – and wondered if they too could hear that which lay beyond the wind; that which hummed and throbbed within his body and yet beyond his body. ... Averi tied the buckle of his sou'wester and was the first to make it to the door.

2

I am in a small room painted green. That is all I know
for my head sears. The only way to describe the pain
is not like a pain at all, rather a blade of light. Nothing
else exists for me in this moment other than the blade,
the green and – now that I blink – the woman standing
at the foot of my bed. She is writing on a clipboard. I
remember her now, of course, as if my memory were
being slowly plugged back in. Her hair is tied back today,
pulled into a girlish ponytail. Once again, I am feeling her
fear hardening like a lattice around her heart. Perhaps
I shall tell her that I understand; that I am holding her
heart as a penguin nestles its young. There is nothing to
fear, I want to tell her. But she blinks hard as she takes
off her glasses, her pen a snap-shut of silence. My eyelids
are so heavy there might be a fat toad sat upon either
of them. Perhaps we shall talk another day. And I pull
those feathers snug around her heart.

That was yesterday. Today the eyes take in the window and its fine mesh grille. Along its left-hand side is a thin strip of slats that offer the only chance of air. Air is not popular in this place, at least not in fresh quantities. I pull the slats to their widest angle and with my nose pressed tight to the metal I breathe air deep into my lungs.

The woman from yesterday is my consultant. I shall not see her for another week. It works that way here. Once a week for one hour and not even guaranteed the same person. But she, at least, is the most consistent. In many ways, in fact. Consistent in her capacity to write notes, for one thing. What a world is missed by the ardent note-taker. But I understand that has become her way. Verbatim seems to be the end-all these days. Another world missed in words.

Reynardo has just come in and asked me if I'd like a cigarette. He comes in several times a day to ask me this question and several times a day I reply that I don't smoke, but that I would be very happy to accompany him. It is a child's delight of a smile. What innocent pleasure he takes in my saying, yes. Dear Reynardo. I don't like to remind him of the routine at the desk.

- Will you come, then?

- Yes, Reynardo, I will come.

I wrap tight my dressing-gown cord, slide my feet into my slippers and follow him out of my room, down the short corridor to the nurses' desk.

Reynardo leans his wide elbows on the plastic counter.

- We want to go for a cigarette, he says.

The nurse, a kind Russian called Dmitri, looks up from his newspaper, congenial, non-committal.

- There is no one, Reynardo, available to take you.

- Really?

- I'm afraid not.

- Oh.

- Shall we come back in an hour, I suggest.

- Yes, Lili, an hour sounds about right, and then we can see who's come on duty, okay?

This is the routine. Reynardo nods. He cannot help but hang his head. He gets but two cigarettes a day if he is lucky. I pat his arm as we walk away from the desk towards the open-plan sitting area.

- How about you show me that card trick, I ask.

How quickly it comes. I have rarely seen such joy in a face, lifting the deep wrinkles of this aged child. Can they not see his purity? The nurses have been instructed not to call him Reynardo nor me Lili. It would only contribute to his pathology, the doctors say. Dmitri was the first to break the rule and now it has become habit. Reynardo is the fox in that wonderful film with Leslie Caron. *Our* Reynardo delights in this most wily of all foxes, and for all the world is in love with Lili.

- Reynardo! I exclaim. How on earth did you do that?

He pulls back the magic card, flicks his eye to the noise of the television, and shuffles his secret to his chest.

3

~**M**ayday, Mayday, Mayday! This is the *Chariot*.
    - Patch, get over here!
    - Mayday, Mayday, Mayday! This is the *Chariot*. Do you read me, over?
    - Get your hand on the throttle.
    - Antenna's down, Skip. There's no radio!
    - We're all going down if you don't help me to turn her.

Patch ran to Averi's side, his hand on the lever. Water broke through the window, right across the wheel, and threw both men against the opposite wall. Averi scrambled, his boots slipping, and pulled Patch up.
    - You okay?
    - I'm okay.

Averi grabbed the wheel as the *Chariot* careered from one side to the other. From every angle water lashed through the wheelhouse. There was no horizon any more, only water piled up like mountain peaks; peaks that collided and pummelled one another.

- Okay, Averi yelled, this is what we're gonna do.

- Skip!

Raul burst into the wheelhouse.

- There's gotta be winds of one hundred and twenty knots out there. We're not gonna make it.

- So clear her, Raul, God dammit. Get the others and clear the deck.

- Jesus, you've gotta be kidding me!

Raul slammed into the side as they toppled to the left. He was staring aghast through the window opposite. A great wall was coming towards them.

- It's gotta be fifty foot, man. *Jesus Christ*, we're not gonna make it.

From down on the deck could just be made out Haiti's shout. He was struggling to lift a huge metal box over the side of the rail. The minute he stood straight a surge knocked him down and slid him into the other side of the boat. Averi turned.

- Raul, listen to me. Listen to me! I can't let go of this wheel, so you gotta go help Trindar and Haiti. You hear me? We're gonna be fine if you clear the deck of all debris and let me and Patch hold her. You got it?

At that moment, something heavy hurtled like a missile towards the window of the wheelhouse, spraying the last pane of glass across the controls.

- Okay, Skip.

- Okay. I need you Raul, so stay sharp.

- Okay, I'm on it.

Averi turned now to the grey barricade. Never in his life had he seen such a height. The only way was to try and spin the *Chariot* to forty-five— Averi stopped. Did he just say *spin*? He looked to Patch, who was shivering and white, both his hands locked on the throttle and poised.

- What's the matter, Skip? We're broadside. You don't wanna turn?

- No.

- *No?*

Averi felt the roll of the swell. The *Chariot* was nose down. Averi loosened his grip on the wheel as another wave shot through and yanked him sideways. Suddenly, the *Chariot* was nose *up*, tilting at such an angle, that Averi could barely keep his footing.

- If we don't turn her, we've had it, Skip.

- Just let her spin, Patch. We gotta let her spin.

- *What?*

Straight away, the wall engulfed them, turning them over like a rolling pin. Averi found himself topside up, his head on the ceiling, gasping as the needle-sharp Atlantic rushed through. But the roll kept momentum until the *Chariot* was right side up, shaking and spewing out surf from every orifice. Averi scrambled across the floor to Patch.

- We're up, we're back up! Take the wheel, okay? I gotta go check the antenna.

Patch whooped and screamed, and then shook his head in complete confusion.

- She spun us, Skip! She spun us!

Averi didn't wait. He pulled himself forward as the *Chariot* lurched, out of the wheelhouse and towards the mast. He could see now that the antenna was hanging down. Averi climbed as the trawler plunged and as the waves soaked him. But no matter how high he climbed he was still no higher than this free-rolling hill range. Waves rose and fell and churned and ate themselves. The wind fed their appetite and they gorged, fat and voracious. And now to the right there was a fresh wave, some thirty feet in height, its top lip curling like a pout.

Averi watched. Another, without water, was flooding his being, flattening all that he knew, spreading his being with silence. Noise raged in Averi's ears, yet somehow he was undisturbed. In the heart of this maelstrom Averi was unafraid. The salt and the bitter cold burned his skin, but Averi was untouched. All the while this silence watched. It watched as he listened, as his body flailed and bounced against the mast, as the spray stung his eyes and choked his throat, as he grappled with the antenna and tried to attach it, as the great thirty-footer crashed starboard to port and threw him to the deck. The boys were screaming and running to help. The silence watched as he lifted his body, as everything dropped and he saw—

Raul was yelling and waving his arms. Did he see it too? And a bundle of chain rope came fly—

4

W hat a joy it is to see the sky. Reynardo has to ask the nurse for a light. She stands inside the corridor that passes, tube-like, from one building to another. She hands out the lighter, Reynardo lights his cigarette, he hands the lighter back; five minutes, she says, before closing the thick glass doors and locking them with her key. This is the procedure, made more tedious by the fact that Reynardo insists on smoking roll-ups which, especially because he is so talkative, have the habit of going out. So involved is he in the to-ings and fro-ings of lighter and roll-up that the sky to him is quite hidden. There is a crystal called blue lace agate, so named for its pale powder blue and delicate filigree of white embroidery. This is the sky today. How softened am I by its beauty. I have forgotten the month, but it feels autumnal; that marvellous sharp kick in the air that sweeps into the lungs and with one burst clears the membranes of that fetid ward.

Reynardo offers me a puff on his cigarette. I smile, but decline. This used to be the drill. Reynardo would either roll me a cigarette, which I would then pretend to light from his, or we would pretend to share just one between us. I would not have been allowed outside otherwise. It is a strange circumstance that to be a smoker is to be permitted the only possibility of freedom for fifteen minutes twice a day. Nowadays, we are beyond pretence. The nurses, at least most of them, know as well as I do that Reynardo is entirely more manageable with his Lili at his side. That's why they turn a blind eye, so that for as long as the game lasts, patient and carer are equal in deception.

It is as well, I suppose, to describe this courtyard of freedom: twelve feet across, a modern red-bricked circle containing two benches, and penned on all sides by the similar red brick of four storeys. It is interesting that someone thought to plant bushes in the thin ring between our pen and the opposite walls. They are neat and parallel and look as if they might have been bought off the rail from a store named Things from Nature. How we insist upon stripping ourselves. It is extraordinary, really. And yet as I say that, there is no judgement. Perhaps you won't believe me, but I am sincere. Judgement left some years ago now. Whatever perceptions arise are much more playful. Humanity must be allowed its teenage tantrum, after all. And besides, this human mind is entirely too reliant on answers. This sky is empty of all answers. How fresh, how free, now that *this* mind knows Nothing.

- What do you mean?
    - Just that.

- That you know nothing?

My consultant is sat in the interview room. The room has been designed for this purpose, though I can't see how. It is a sparse, grey-walled box with a circular grey plastic table in front of a small meshed window that overlooks the next block. It makes quite clear the medical interest in the human mind.

- I don't understand. Doctor Kolinsky – that is her name – is holding her glasses in front of her chest, twiddling them back and forth. Are you trying to avoid talking?

- No, of course not.

- But to suggest that you know nothing supposes one of two things. Either that you feel accused of a crime to which either your innocence or guilt has pressed you, out of anxiety, to say that you know nothing; or it communicates to me that you have nothing of interest to say and are in fact showing your displeasure of this whole procedure.

I feel her anger, keenly. No words of answer come, except a momentary thought, a wish rather, that I might appease her. It dispels as quickly as it appeared, for clearly it is not up to me. I recognise that silence shall confirm her suspicion. But there is nothing to do: it fills the room, swelling this being with beauty.

My eye meets her eye. Hers is blue and so fearful that, if I were allowed, I should wrap her small frame within mine. I know now that even if I were allowed, this is not always appropriate. The embrace takes place inwardly instead. For how can it be helped when all you see is beauty?

Her eye darts away and finds root in her clipboard. What a frenzy meets her pen. Those words at her disposal shall have immense power and shall heed warning, most decidedly, that I am not helping myself.

A length of hair drops loose from behind this doctor's ear. It lies with its reddish tinge like a veil across her cheek. A ponytail is by far the better option. Then we at least stand a chance.

5

What an appearance of white there was. Strangely, it had the effect of stretching space back into itself so that there was no sense of where space ended or began. Averi heard a voice and then alongside of it came a face so close he almost screamed. The voice nonetheless had a gentle quality, though its words were indistinct. More white of a white coat, followed by the blinding shock of a torchlight in his eye. It was then he felt the pain, a pain so numbing it reached into his brain and rendered it mute. Nothing was known except the feeling of his body supported on this bed, the whiteness of those infinite walls and the pain. A new voice, recognisable somehow, appeared to be speaking about pain. At least, all that was heard was this final word, leaping out to him as the only coherence. The white of the white coat receded and was replaced by the darkness of night. Hair as smooth and as dark as her skin. Averi smiled as he focused on Nyx.

- Where are the boys?

- They didn't leave your side for three days, Averi. This morning the doctor insisted they go. It's a wonder you didn't wake from their noise. They'll be back tomorrow.

Averi could feel the heat of tears brimming. He did not know exactly why he should cry, but that they had been here – Patch, Haiti, Raul and Trindar – was too tender to bear. Yet he knew this was only the surface; a catalyst of fine proportion. Averi couldn't have contained himself if he tried. What a well of things he did not rightly know or understand. He couldn't even have described it as sorrow, rather an unlocking that broke all levies. It didn't make any sense to him why; only that the last few days had to have something to do with it. He was vaguely aware that figures were gathering. He felt himself lift his body upright so that his lungs might expand to each sob. He was vaguely aware that the figures dispersed as quickly as they had gathered, but that Nyx remained at his side.

The white room had begun to undress itself and Averi could now make out his surroundings. He was sat upright in the corner bed of a bright ward containing a dozen similar beds. On the opposite wall were two double sets of floor-to-ceiling windows that looked out onto broad lawns and fine mature trees charged with the insatiable red and russet of Fall. Breath caught itself in Averi's chest; that familiar childish intake as he stilled. He saw that the men in the opposite beds were watching. One smiled and then dropped his chin into his magazine. It was then that Averi remembered, and he lifted his hand to his head and to the thick bandage that encased it. Not, that is to say, how he came to be bandaged, but that moment before blackout, the moment when he saw—

Averi turned to Nyx.

He saw her gaze, her large, almond-shaped eyes the colour of walnut. He saw how still she sat, her hands resting palm to palm on her crossed knee as if they were cupping a secret. His lungs felt full and rested, without yearning of any kind. The pain in his head was there, but it did not trouble him.

- Welcome home, said Nyx.

And this time tears fell silently.

6

The daily round of this place is as follows. Wake-up call is at seven-thirty by the nurse on night duty, the level of morning greeting varying with each mood and personality. Dmitri's is a gentle, reassuring knock. Anastasia, on the other hand, generally blasts open each door along the corridor with a wide bark for all; while little Mareka, who is still finding her way, is of no use to the drugged sleep of these inmates. Her timid, apologetic knock accompanied by her delicate, pointed features put me in mind of a dormouse discovering for the first time that it is prey. I have only to smile and to wish her good morning for her entire demeanour to melt. The wake-up call is the last job of the night staff. Eight o'clock breakfast, which we are strongly encouraged to attend, is supervised by the day shift. Today is Monday, which means Anastasia with a weekend back story. This she shall trawl around on her wide haunches as a dare to anyone who opposes her. If there were ever a mission anywhere it would be to extract a smile from this troubadour of woe. I once called her this to her face, but I don't quite think she caught the irony. Dearest Anastasia, if only you knew that your litany of troubles are but the stuff of dreams. But then, that might be the lyric for us all.

Normally on Mondays we are scheduled for the morning arts and crafts class in the old building. But a notice has gone up on the board that a tap was left running in a blocked sink and has flooded the workshop. The implication is that one of us is responsible. This seems unlikely, especially since this two-hour slot on a Monday morning is the only opportunity – saving smokers' breaks – we on Saffron Ward get to leave these stuffy confines. That anyone would sabotage this rare escape stretches the bounds of possibility. The most obvious culprit is Ashton, the cleaner who – bless his heart – would not know a bottle of bleach if you pressed it under his nose. This is not said to be unkind. On the contrary, Ashton is an inspired romantic who mixes Tennyson with drum and bass. One day he let me listen to his creation on his MP3 player. I have to say it was haunting. What a wonderful display of the infinite possibilities of creation we are. Such perfection passes through these corridors. Perfection albeit veiled by layers of belief. If only they knew of their own Perfection they should not suffer so. But still, this is quite as it should be. Each story contains its own opportunity for freedom, and each story must unfold as many twists and turns as is necessary in order finally to wipe clear the screen of delusion.

Twelve o'clock is meds time. I am on risperidone and lithium; an anti-psychotic and a mood stabiliser. This subject is bound to resurface. Right now, words do not come, except the obvious: far too many questions are left unanswered. And my goodness, what a wasted opportunity. There shall be plenty occasion to explore this minefield, but for now I feel compelled to return to safe territory: lunchtime and its twelve-thirty serving.

Food, I think it fair to say, is less than inspiring. All twelve patients of Saffron Ward eat together in the dining room, a glass-walled partitioned area that doubles as a meeting or writing room. We sit four to a table and more often than not among the same four. My table comprises Reynardo, myself, Sarah and Jude. It is a challenge to sit beside Reynardo on many counts. To begin with, food brings out an irrepressible excitement in him. Talking is his most favourite occupation, after of course watching his favourite film. Put food in the equation and there is no silencing him. I am more than happy to listen, for his childlike awe at the sight of whatever is dumped before him, is enchanting. It almost makes me believe that for one delicious moment we have been treated to a luncheon worthy of Michelin success. Sarah and Jude make their annoyance known, but have never tried to move on to another table. Perhaps because none of the other inmates will tolerate Reynardo's *spitting*. He is, without exaggeration, quite the worst eater I have ever seen, and it is a rare day when my plate is not rained on with spittle. Needless to say what was already inedible is quickly beyond mention. The nurses have noted my reluctance to eat as a sign of *disorder* and have reported it accordingly. I could try to explain, but dearest Reynardo, I cannot bear to see his distress. For move him they shall and he shall cry those heart-rending sobs of a lost child. Far better I give in to the innermost mound of food on my plate and hope for the best.

After lunch is free time, an interestingly termed section of the day. Those with special privileges may use this time to go outside, to the shop or the park. But no one on our ward has special privileges at the moment. Sarah did for one day. But then it was discovered she had tried to bite a homeless guy and was brought back to hospital by the police, who made it very clear that she should not be allowed out again until her biting habits were under control. No one ever asked *why* Sarah had attempted to eat a homeless guy. Merely she was to be punished by loss of privileges and a higher dose of lithium. Reynardo has never yet earned one day outside in the whole time he has been here. It is because he refuses to respond to any other name; or indeed to address me as anything other than Lili. Admonitions are wasted while these characters serve a purpose. I am happy to be Lili for as long as he needs her. This and my apparent reticence to eat and to talk are what deprive me of *my* special privileges.

Luckily, my imagination is keen. I can rustle up a May Day glory quicker than you can blink. How boldly those springtime colours cavort: *Hyacinthoides non-scripta*, the English bluebell. The forest floor is thick with their elegant droop, their delicate petals rolling back on themselves to soak in those token rays; a little to the right and I can take the path leading out of the wood. It is springy to step and the air is streaked with moss and fern, until at last I emerge in a field that is rippled with life: meadow buttercup, ox-eye daisy, red clover, self-heal and yarrow. Butterflies dance their springtime love trysts - the swallowtail, the small tortoiseshell and the green-veined white; fat bumbles sink into clover and the air is a symphony. Is that a willow warbler, its high note tumbling down scale? Real or imagined, I know that both are mere dream. On the rare occasion that words do come, such truth has found expression. But this, too, has kept me without privileges.

In any case, those of Saffron Ward spend their afternoons either in their rooms or in the tiny open-plan sitting area. Here we have a television that remains on all day whether it is watched or not. There are board games and a chess board and an area to make tea. At four o'clock biscuits or the occasional cake arrive. Incidentally, there are not enough seats to accommodate twelve, but by happy chance we have never yet congregated en masse in front of the television. Perhaps because the inmates are not naturally sociable. There is a tendency for these beings to hibernate. It is obvious the moment you encounter them that they have retreated far beneath the layers of their own skin, to a place utterly secret. To attempt to pierce this hibernation is an act of trespass. These beings may know nothing but winter, but nevertheless they are experts of their own terrain, and intruders would do well to honour that.

Supper is at six, bed at ten. Between the narrow corridor connecting the rooms and the nurses' desk, between the sitting area and the dining room we must have paced a thousand miles. These are our walls, among many admittedly. Low-ceilinged, closed-windowed, grey and cramped. I once heard a visitor of the sane kind suggest that this ward was a place in which to go mad. How I smiled. At least someone was beginning to see the irony. Life has certainly tossed us a curve-ball. And how grateful I am. To be here in the midst of winter and to see such beauty. What greater privilege than that?

7

There was almost no impulse to move. Averi did not know how many days he had lain. The pain in his head had subsided, but what remained was worse: a fatigue so enervating his limbs felt weighted to the bed. It was curious that his senses were nonetheless sharp. Why, he wondered, should fatigue not dampen his sense of smell, for example? Yet here it was, heightened to the point of exhaustion. And not just *one* sense; that might have been bearable. He was crowded on all sides by smell, taste, sound and light. Colours felt like sordid intrusions; the stench of bonfire, sidling in, was acrid and rasping on the back of his throat; seagulls, involved in some fracas, were aiming their rude shouts like darts; and the strangest taste of something metallic on his tongue sickened his empty stomach.

When was the last time he had eaten? Hunger felt like a foreign land, coupled with laughter and conversation and the success of a good haul. The boys had stopped calling and were no doubt resigned to the catch without their skipper. In the days immediately after the hospital they had attempted to visit several times a day. The *Chariot* must have sat idle a whole week. They had knocked, sang, cajoled, tried to force windows, until eventually Averi had heard Haiti calling them away. It was not their place to push, he'd said, when pushing was not wanted. For a few days more they had tried their last chance on the telephone. Averi could not think of it. Their voices on the telephone machine repeated in his mind: Haiti's muscular bass betraying his concern, Raul's high-pitched impatience, Patch's jovial plea. Even dear Trindar, distrusting of words, never mind telephone machines, had forced himself to announce his name, to then remain for a full minute in silence. There was only one voice Averi would have listened to, but that did not come.

With the greatest effort Averi turned onto his side and faced the window. This view had always been a joy. Today it merely was as it was. The decking, the terrace that sloped down, and the ocean beyond. The boys had always joked that Averi had designed the ocean along with his house. Certainly, it was not possible to separate them. The outside walls of both bedroom and living room were entirely of glass. How many times had Averi awakened in this bed, his nose pressed against the glass, to wonder for a sleepy moment whether he were under the sky or under his roof? Not even this thought came today. Only oblivion, pulling him down like an anchor to the seabed.

At that moment, his eye caught the blue beech at the corner of his vision. Its leaves were almost shed. The chestnut, the maple and, further down the hill, the great Bebb's Oak, were all of them close to bereft. What a strange description! Averi had never considered the winter trees as bereft. Now they were stripped, blunted, exposed. Fear shot through like a warning. But fear of what? Averi had not the will to find answers. He remembered quite clearly the fanfare of the hospital grounds, and now look! All he could deduce was that he must have lain since then, unkempt, unwashed and unshaven for at least a month. Averi ran his fingers across his cheek. He did not dare to see himself in the mirror, for he knew that what should look back would in no way resemble his former self.

8

Her name is Katherine. I should say she looks like a Katherine, if ever a Katherine were to have a look. 'Katherine' is distinguished and erudite; it has the smug musicality of three knowing syllables. The knowing of intellect and of all things orderly. It is the dowager of female suffrage, wearing its hard-won flag of independence with sedate but proud colours. This one, rather less advanced in years – not much beyond thirty, I should imagine – squirms in her seat, and then looks at me over her glasses. I have to say I can hardly blame her.

- Why the sudden interest in my name?

For the first time since we have begun our talks, Doctor Kolinsky looks me wholly in the eye. It is not a look of meeting, however; rather of defiance and I understand why. She thinks I am trying to turn tables and dissect *her*. I regret now my playfulness. It was not planned or manipulated. I saw that *K* and innocently asked if she might tell me her name. And besides, it seems strange after months of sitting this way that she should know mine and I not know hers.

- I'm sorry. I didn't mean to upset you.

This is something I am beginning to recognise. This personality, this *me*, enjoys words. Rather too much, in fact. Before, they were my currency. I was able to negotiate all manner of highways on the back of these red devils. What satisfaction, indeed joy, was to be found in understanding their myriad layers; their untapped connotations. Even something as innocuous as a name.

- Words can be a trap.

- What do you mean 'a trap'?

- When we hold on too tight and imagine they are true. But, there are other times when there is no choice but to let them come. Only then might we be certain of their truth.

This last one – *truth* – hangs in the air for several breaths. I see that it has caught her unawares, as if she were not sure what to do with it.

- To be sure, I say. Words are this one's learning.

- This one?

- This *me*.

- As opposed to another *me*?

- As opposed to *your* 'me'.

Katherine still holds my eye, quizzical this time, as if I were a rare specimen. There is less irritation, less anxiety, but distrust nonetheless. It pervades her entire form; distrust for me, distrust for herself. I have a sense she is not yet happy in her face, but it is a lovely face. Pale skin of the Irish kind, and those eyes, that blue of cornflowers.

- I still don't understand, she says. You speak objectively, as if you were something outside of your 'me'.

I cannot help but smile. How wonderful.

- Not outside, I reply. *Before*.

This smile is so broad it fills the room. Indeed it cannot fill it for it *is* the room; nor is it contained by our grey-walled box; for there is nothing but smile. Dearest Katherine, if you could only see what I see.

She has reached for her pen, which has so far lain untouched. This makes me wonder why she has been wearing her glasses all this time. Normally they wait for the pen. Colour has raised her cheekbones, and I notice a tic at her left temple. She writes and I watch. Her lips are pursing ever so slightly and for the first time I wonder what thoughts are forming her sentences.

- It's strange, I say, that I have never been curious before about what you write, about *your* words.

This realisation is something of a shock. For months now what had hitherto defined this personality has not so much as raised an eyebrow. I have watched with curiosity the vehemence of her pen, but have had no interest in its output. It is as if all identification with that facet had been thrown away, effortlessly. Today, curiosity has returned, but with none of its bite. I wonder if it would be possible to explain this to my doctor of psychiatry. What was once so personal may now again be so, but without my being personally attached to it. Once more, I cannot help but smile. So much has been dropped and now this most tenacious of attachments.

- The writer may write but is no longer a writer.

The playfulness of it all suddenly makes me laugh.

- I'm sorry?

- Forgive me.

- What's so funny?

- It all is. It's all so cheeky. So ridiculously playful!

I just can't stop. I know I must look ridiculous, but this laughter keeps coming, so much that tears start to run.

Doctor Kolinsky stares at me, impassive, and then drops once more to her notepad. It strikes me that it cannot be amusing to be outside of the joke. I should so love to share it with her, but I know for now I must find another way. I calm myself and let a few moments of quiet sit between us.

- May I read what you write?

- I don't think that would be helpful.

- Why not? Can you not see how it sits there between us?

- What does?

- The very act of your note-taking. If I am never privy to your conclusions then how can we know where we both are? If I were to sit here making notes about you, would you not feel cut off?

- What would you like to write about me?

I see how she is drawing me away from my line of argument. I am not interested in that deception. I nod, and look down to my lap. I know that she does not wish to deceive me. The whole point is that Katherine believes quite earnestly that she is doing the right thing. Or rather – she *had* believed she was doing the right thing. This is where her confusion lies: I know that in sitting with me on and off for nearly eleven months her layers have begun to loosen. They are far from being shed, but loosened enough to cast her adrift for one hour a week; to cause her to wonder if she has the faintest notion about anything any more. The fear that arises out of this question is causing her to reach haphazardly for tried and tested ways. I see her struggle, and so genuinely wish I could reassure her. Unfortunately, for now, we cannot get beyond pathology.

- Speaking of names, she says, why do you still insist upon being called Lili?

- I don't insist.

- The nurses inform me that you refuse to be called by your own name.

- That's not true.

- Did I not address you as Lili, at your prompting, at the beginning of this session?

- Yes, you did, but for the reason that when I arrived Reynardo—

- Who you persistently encourage—

- Was still here. I didn't realise your session with him hadn't finished. I've told you before; I only ask to be called Lili as long as he is in earshot. As it happens, on any other occasion, I don't mind what name you call me. It's simply that some of the nurses have taken to calling me Lili out of habit.

- Do you not consider it harmful?

- How so?

- That you willingly support Reynardo's – Bill's – delusion.

- He has created it for a reason. And as long as it helps him I have to go along with it. He must peel away his ... delusions ... in his own time. If I rush him and denude him of his only joy, I shall also take away his only support.

I understand I must sound to her like an insufferable know-it-all, but truly, how else to explain my reasoning? Tears prick at my eyeballs. We seem always to reach this impasse.

Katherine closes the file, puts both clipboard and pen on the table, and slides them slightly away from her. I see that anger has braised those cheekbones.

- For someone who has been silent so long, she says, you have much to say today.

- I don't wish to upset you, really I don't. But as I said before, sometimes words must come.

It has started to rain outside. Large globules, fat against the pane. It feels for a moment as if Katherine and I were two fish stuck in a goldfish bowl whose water is thick with algae. Cannot everyone see that all sense is suffocating? The rain is the first sign of clean reason. I reach forward and slide the clipboard and my file across the table. How curious to see my name typed in bold on the front cover, as if the words scribed within were the summation of this character they now call Lili.

I turn the cover. The first page is my admittance. January the ninth.

I look up and see that Katherine has removed her glasses. How chastened I am to be genuinely surprised. The glasses have been placed on the table, her hands are in her lap and those cornflowers are fearful, but willing.

9

This section of the beach was a storehouse. Great rocks that had been washed ashore in a former age lay scattered like hillocks. As a boy Averi had imagined they were giant tortoises sleeping after an impossibly long journey. He would climb on their backs and listen to their adventures. It had seemed amazing to him that they had seen such fascinating and foreign lands, but yet returned in their old age to this island of their birth. Afterwards came the search for treasure, for fossils and shells, and Averi would collect with the connoisseur's nose the delicate white angel's eye, the secretive cowrie with its thin stretch of mouth, and his favourite, the jagged and pronged spider conch. He had been absorbed and yet saddened by this graveyard of the sea. And so he gave them all names and led them on fine sea-faring expeditions so that they should not forget the way of the ocean.

Averi looked out to the wide stretch of low tide. All this he thought he knew. He did not inhale if the sea did not inhale; he did not exhale unless the sea exhaled. Their symbiosis had been complete. And now – now Averi was reminded of a young man from a nearby village who had been tossed by a wave and left a cripple. Old folk said he must have angered the wave, but Averi knew this was not true. Sometimes the sea rises this way. It had simply caught the boy unawares, lifted him like a plaything, landed him upside down and broken his neck. All at once, Averi felt a hot line of rage from his gut to his throat. To see the flat calm now – so unassuming, so innocent – and to know of its opposite filled Averi with incomprehension, with a rage at the sheer randomness, the futility, the ugly, capricious nature of it all. For it was no exaggeration: the ocean, his great mother, father and teacher, whom he had loved more than his own self, had finally broken him, too. Averi threw away his shells and cried his rage into his hands.

Perhaps several minutes had passed, for Averi was forced to blink against the sun when he lifted his head. Two children, the Boaeker boys, were standing some feet away, their collection box filled with trophies. Maybe they were embarrassed to see a grown man cry, and especially the skipper. All summer they had trailed at Averi's heel, peppered him with questions, and had begged to be taken on a catch. Now they looked to their own heels, the elder boy nudging his brother.

- Pop says you's lucky to be alive, Skip.

- Uh huh, said the other.

- You's all lucky, really. We was making a collection, Skip, since we know how much you love 'em.

The boys looked to one another and then back to Averi.

- Okay, Skip, said the eldest. We're gonna leave 'em right here for you. The boy put down the tin box and then edged back. We're ready to go on a catch whenever you are.

The youngest boy looked up to his brother as if unsure of this last statement. The elder shrugged and made a face to silence him.

- We'll be seeing you, Skip. We're ready when you are.

Clearly, the boys were uncertain what might be best in this situation. They lingered on their parting, as if hoping Averi might suddenly surprise them.

Averi witnessed the whole scene without even a longing to comfort them. Impassively, he watched them go, their little shoulders hunched forward as they discussed their fallen hero.

- How long, do you think, 'til you're ready?

Averi lurched inside. He turned his head sharply in the opposite direction. She was sat not six feet away on a flat-topped rock, with the sun upon her head.

- Nyx!

Then came her smile. Even in shadow, Averi could see that it filled the sky.

- It's good to see you, Averi.

10

⚘

Averi found himself looking to his toes, waiting for something more. The inward lurch was gnawing now, throbbing his stomach until it burned. It was no use sitting. This anger had to move, to tread fast, back and forth; it resolved to leave, it rounded back on itself; it was so loud he no longer heard the gulls and the children.

- Averi?

Was she not in the least bit concerned? Was there to be no word of explanation for her month of absence? Had she forced a path to his front door and demanded to know if he were eating, sleeping, *breathing*? He knew without looking up that she sat there, still as the deep, oblivious to his suffering.

- You are angry with me.

Averi heard himself snort through his nose. He turned his back to her, not quite the full degree, but three-quarters at least.

- I see that you are, and I'm sorry for it. But, I'm not going to lie to you or say pretty things to make you feel better. I had to follow your lead on this, Averi.

- *Follow my lead?* Fury at last bellowed out. What do you mean follow my lead? Do you have any idea what I've been through? It doesn't even make sense that we survived that storm. We had one hundred and twenty knots of wind out there. I almost died, Nyx. How about you follow that one. *I almost died!*

- How fortunate you are.

As if a needle had punctured both lungs, Averi sat on a rock, winded. He shook his head and stared as if she were mad.

- What a rare gift. To die before you die. It is the *only* gift and the only reason you are here. But you wish me to commiserate over details. Certainly I can do that. Forgive me if I miss a piece. I trust that you shall prompt me when I stray. There was a storm at sea. It was so localised that we on shore got but a small taste of it. The *Chariot* was unable to navigate. Thirty-foot waves were swamping her. There was little you boys could do save bail for all you were worth. You lost radio contact. While you were trying to reattach the antenna, one of those waves threw you off the mast and down to the deck. You might easily have broken your back; instead, a huge coil of chain rope came flying and struck you a devastating blow to the back of the head. After which the storm passed over, allowing the boys to steer you home.

A gull at that moment landed between them. Averi and Nyx watched as it strutted back and forth, as it pecked for offerings among the pebbles. Averi had never been fond of gulls, finding them boisterous and hectoring. Today, he had no feelings towards them, none whatsoever. He did not even wish to have feelings. He stared at the creature as he stared at himself, benumbed and exhausted.

Having not found what he was looking for, the bird stretched open his wings and gave a shrill cry. Perhaps he was warning his friends that this place was a dead loss for pickings. He lifted himself up and in the few seconds it took to take flight, Averi witnessed a strange sight. The sun must have created an optical illusion for in that compressed moment of time he saw Nyx *through* the seagull. It was as if they had been fused, as if a transparent gull had somehow been superimposed on her face. In a flash both bird and image had gone and all that remained was the Nyx that he knew. Averi shivered. The November wind had begun to stir and had found its way through the neck of his wind-breaker. Never mind optical illusions, what of his own image? What a pitiful sight he must look, a huddled frame of a once strong physique bent double on a windswept beach, eyes red from crying and a heart empty of feeling. Even a cool rendition of his near-death experience did not stir him. From somewhere at least rose a smile, albeit a smile of disbelief. In Nyx's eye it softened. Not enough to bring back feeling, but enough to lay down defence. Averi was too shattered to know anything any more.

- Shall we walk?

It seemed miraculous that he was even capable of that.

At the top of the dunes lay Martia's, a white-slatted, sea-beaten, low-eaved pit-stop for walkers and beach-combers. Other proprietors closed for the winter, but Martia had a stout nose for the islanders and their ways. She knew on a chilled November afternoon they would rather seek out her fireside than their own, to sip their thoughts in a hot whisky or a milky chocolate. She did not interfere or offer up much in the way of conversation, but for that her customers were grateful. She slid now two mugs of coffee and a jug of steamed milk across the counter, and a tray of thin gingers. Averi saw her and Nyx exchange a smile. He knew it was for him, but he could not respond. He moved instead to the fireplace and to the warm red seats either side of it. What relief it was to settle in the heat, to sit and stare at the flames.

Nyx was taking off her coat and her woollen jerkin beneath. Her hair fell loose and knotted out of her hat. Averi turned back to the fire. He did not understand why it was suddenly so difficult to look at her. He remembered how when she had first arrived in Quartermaine he had been so completely tongue-tied. He remembered how easily she had dispelled his nerves, until they had been happy to sit for hours together in both silence and in talk. And yet, impatience had always surrounded him. A longing that gnawed to the marrow.

- You confused that longing with me, Averi.

Averi shot Nyx a look, startled by her insight. Not that he should be. It was her tendency to speak as if she were privy to his innermost thoughts. It was both alarming and a comfort. Today, however, it only angered him more.

- Do you remember I once said we shall meet when you no longer need me?

Averi did remember. He squirmed in his chair. Again tears pricked the innards of his eyes. It was so revolting to be this weeping invalid.

- I didn't understand then, and I don't understand now, he replied.

- Hmm.

There was a spit from the fire as a coal splint came loose from the grating. Nyx leaned forward and with the end of the poker carefully nudged it back into place. The firelight played on her face, a dance of possibility. Suddenly, Averi felt sunk in such beauty, he could barely breathe. Tears came out of him, for there was no stopping them.

- We could try to understand together, she said.

How gently she spoke without plea. She sat back in her chair and sipped at her coffee. Waiting with infinite patience. Averi caught her eye and saw in its impish glint the playfulness of love. He felt then, and this was the only way he could describe it, a great emptying, as if his intestines had just dropped out from beneath him; as if weighted shackles had slipped to the floor. He wiped his face with the heel of his hand.

- I don't understand anything anymore.

- Now that sounds hopeful.

Averi exhaled a smile through his nose. He looked over his knuckles that were holding his chin and shook his head. Nyx smiled back, raising her eyebrows. For a moment, that old spark of cheekiness that had been his way wanted to express itself: a self-deprecating joke, a life-belittling aside. His tongue had just about formed one before Nyx cut him off.

- You know, in times such as these the best thing you can do is throw yourself into the fire.

Averi stopped. His mouth shut and he was silent.

11

Admitted January ninth amid acute psychotic episode and full psychotic breakdown. Strong bipolar tendency; delusional; possible borderline schizophrenia.

Entry for January twenty-eighth: Patient refuses to speak; according to nurses almost entirely silent since the first week of admittance. Reaction to Canada; seemed surprised to be questioned, but no verbal response. GP notes indicate sharp weight loss over short space of time, though no displays of unusually abnormal behaviour over food. Periods stopped for three months last year. GP notes highlight alternating euphoria and despair. Patient refusal to take anti-depressant medication. Continues to stay in her room most of the time; this session conducted in Patient's room.

Entry for February eleventh: Patient refuses all medication; no violent behaviour, consistent with all previous behaviour, nonetheless 'politely' refuses on numerous counts. Speaking today, but only in response to simple questioning. She does not appear to move from her corner of the bed, but stares ahead of her, eyes down, as if in some sort of 'meditation' or trance. When asked if that is what she is doing, she did engage eye contact with me very briefly, and answered 'no'. Her expression is of someone who considers they know more than we do. She smiles a great deal, despite her very lethargic energy. Forcibly injected with depot. Depot injection to continue fortnightly indefinitely.

March eighteenth: delusions of grandeur. Patient claims her 'discovery' is the most important discovery of the human race. She does not want to say yet what this discovery is. When asked if she is the only person to have made this discovery, Patient replies, of course not, but – verbatim – 'it seems to be a rare being that does'. Today is the first time she has used the expression 'discovery'; seems to have something to do with alter ego. This becomes clear when alter ego makes an appearance towards the end of the session. It is male, no doubt expressing repressed animus. The details of his world are precise. When alter ego is challenged, Patient regresses to silence. This male persona is clearly undergoing an emotional breakdown of some sort.

April twenty-second: delusions of grandeur. Today made a comment about doctors' pictures on name badges. Clearly at odds with authority. Enjoys staring at doctors; effect is to unnerve and maintain her autonomy. No visible anger; clearly repressed. Taken to sitting for hours, cross-legged, on bed. Some sort of 'spiritual' delusion continues.

May twenty-seventh: alter ego spoke for entire hour; 'he' – the fisherman – appears to be expressing his own psychotic breakdown. He responds well to questioning. A second aspect, this time female, is now appearing alongside the male aspect. 'She' seems to be the one to whom 'he' defers. Patient continues to complain of side effects to depot. Prescribed procyclidine to counter effects of stiffness and loss of muscle control. Considering switch from depot injection to oral meds: risperidone.

June tenth: Patient seems to think she is some sort of 'Buddha' (my description). Returned now to near-permanent silence. Refuses to join in activities or partake in social engagements with other patients. Engaged in full-time 'meditation'. Continued denial of psychosis. Wrote on paper that we are all delusional. Patient considers doctors to be more delusional than she. Refuses to be drawn again on Canada.

July first: Patient alternately laughing and crying. Seems to be talking in riddles. Main interest is what she terms the Self. Patient claims that her mind is all lies and that there is 'not one ounce of truth in her mind' (her words). Delusions of grandeur again. She claims to 'know truth', but had admitted two seconds earlier there was no truth in her. Considers herself privy to some sort of private truth that we are all unaware of.

August twelfth: Patient used the expression 'godly principle', and then seemed to withdraw when probed on it. Patient remarked that she would prefer the same doctor each week. When told that this was not always possible she was polite, respectful, even kind. This describes all her communications. Patient complaining of drowsiness in the mornings. Good sleep, but erratic energy levels. Claims meds are causing pain in her joints and 'uncomfortable-ness' in her skin. Side effects to procyclidine: dizziness, dry mouth and blurred vision.

August nineteenth: reaction to first ECT = expected headaches and further retreat. Continued disinterest in discussing this method of treatment.

September sixteenth: Patient tells me that she is not responsible for her life. When asked to explain, her language becomes poetic. It is difficult to get beneath the riddle and see what she is saying. Patient is clever with words and uses them to distance our progress. She has become friends with a new patient, Bill. He insists on calling her Lili. Patient does not wish to contradict him. I point out that this will hamper his recovery. Patient is listless today. Patient unable to separate what happens in the world with what happens in her. Classic schizophrenic symptom of belief in 'signs'. She speaks of consciousness and awareness and that there are no such things as miracles. In her words: 'Miracles are only miracles to the unaware.' When asked what she means by the term 'unaware', she answers 'all those who have not yet awakened to their true nature'. I ask if she thinks she has awakened, she says 'to awaken is to *not* think. Awakening is just the first step'. I ask what she means by 'true nature'. She replies, 'merely to know that you are'. Can't decide if she is being deliberately obtuse. As for the 'signs' and visions that she claims to see, I suggest to her that they may not be real. Her answer is: 'Of course, not absolutely real. But anything can manifest relatively.' She seems to believe that she is privy to an entirely different universe of knowledge (my terminology). Considering a switch of anti-psychs. Round three ECT.

October seventh: suggest to Patient that she work towards understanding her pathology. Patient writes, 'this so-called pathology is both a lie and my path home.' Example of Patient's use of poetic language to confuse and maintain control of the session. She sits with eyes closed for the rest of the session. On my suggestion that she is a 'fraud', she responds with: 'Of course, and so are you.' I do not see any progress or willingness to cooperate.

November eleventh: Patient diverts the attention once more away from her and on to me. More undermining in an effort to show me that I cannot help her, e.g. belittling my name. By calling me by my first name she puts me down a peg and strips me of authority and any medical knowledge. N.B. Must raise authority issue. By her own admission she points out her own manipulation of words. Very talkative today, as if a light had been switched back on. But once again reverts to game-playing, laughing at private jokes, and poetic, pseudo-spiritual talk to show that she is beyond my capabilities of understanding. Is committed to her new identity of Lili. Refuses to back down on this. Another means of distancing herself and preventing me from discovering her real identity. Still not volunteering any more comments on the Canadian alter egos. Talkative patch is possible indication of acute manic phase. Prescribed higher lithium concentration.

There are so many pages; these are just a selection picked at random. I close the file and slide it into the middle of the table. My goodness, will this rain ever stop? It is a deluge, hammering tooth and nail at this fishbowl.

- Katherine, may I tell you a story?

I look up and see that Doctor Kolinsky has not moved one inch, though she perhaps has paled and is as blank as I. She does not answer, but waits patiently.

- One day, I begin, a young woman was travelling alone in the great subcontinent of Southern India. While sat in a taxi-cab amid the hooters and claxons of small-town India, and the dust and motorcycles and the blistering heat, she was struck by a vision of the island of

Iona, a picturesque spot off the west coast of Scotland. It was not the first time the vision had come. Over the last few days the young woman had been increasingly sensing that she was being called there, that she must cut short her travels and return to the home of her relatives. It was not entirely clear why, and since this feeling seemed so random and at odds with her current situation, her mind was quick to dismiss it.

However, on this particular morning the feeling had returned with uncommon bite, and a deep knowing arose that to Iona she must go. At that moment, she looked out of the taxi-cab window and stared aghast: a rickshaw van was riding so close she could almost touch it, and on its side was strapped a wooden board, upon which in enormous black letters was written the word 'Iona'. Needless to say, the young woman was immediately convinced of this sign and all plans were set in motion.

Now, it was this young woman's experience that the mind was a mischievous monkey. She might have predicted that in the course of time it would reject this knowing as mere invention, and despite her intuitive understanding that this was the mind's inherent tendency, she had by the end of two weeks rejected all plans for Iona. That is until the following event. It was to pass that on a similar car-ride – although this time on a deserted road in deepest Tamil country, with that irrepressible 'God's green' of the rice fields flashing by on either side – the vision and feeling of Iona appeared before her once again. And this time most decidedly, as if it were shaking her by the intestine and demanding her attention. For there came at that moment a very sorry-looking rickshaw van, this one piled high with coconuts, upon whose roof was nailed a huge placard on which, it might be guessed, was scribed 'Iona'. The result: flights were changed and booked, and Iona was visited for several weeks, during which time it became beautifully apparent why she was meant to be there.

Katherine is blinking, several times in quick succession. She uncrosses her legs, and crosses them again on the opposite side. A wind has lifted now and is forcing great swathes of rain to batter the glass at an angle. The light has dimmed and the moment is so present we can touch it.

- According to this, I say, with my hand reaching towards the closed file, such an experience may be termed as a schizophrenic or psychotic delusion. Is that right?

- Yes.

- That in fact there were no rickshaw vans, only a heavily charged imagination.

- Yes.

- That there was no inner knowing to go to Iona, only an idea that became part of an increasing delusion.

- Yes.

Katherine nods, and then I nod back.

My heart breaks for her to see what I see.

Suddenly, Katherine takes a large, involuntary breath. I have noticed this before with surprise, for I have this tendency, too. There is a name for it, but I have no idea what it is. Often people think it is a breath of impatience or boredom, but far from it. It is rather as if the lungs had been holding on to some thought for a while, and suddenly with the greatest relief, broaden for a wide intake. Since it is involuntary she is quite unselfconscious about it. How strange that this seeing should become the trigger: I feel a spring snap, and there is absolutely nothing I can do about it. This entire body is a deep contraction. These tears have no limit. As potent as that barrage at the window. At some point it is even a struggle to breathe, for convulsions like these are not discreet; they require absolute surrender.

I notice that Katherine is finding it hard to look at me. She has leaned her elbow on the arm of her chair and is rubbing her lips with the backs of her fingernails. How delicate she is. I feel her heart as it flutters like trapped wings. Hand it over, dearest Katherine, I long to say. How safe you are, and you don't even know it.

We sit there together in the dim light far beyond the allotted hour. My chest catches for some while yet, as we bask, empty, in silence.

PART TWO

1

~**C**an you tell me what they look like?

Averi leaned forward, elbows on knees, and rubbed his face with his hands. He was not entirely comfortable talking about this.

- They don't look like anything. I don't know what they look like. I don't see them.

- You hear them?

- No, they speak, but it's *me* who speaks as them.

Averi looked up and caught Nyx's eye. There was too much kindness there to know what she was thinking.

- Are they here now, she asked.

- No, it's not like that.

- What is it like?

- They speak when I don't think about them.

- And how long have they been coming?

- I dunno. Since I was three, maybe four, I guess. You think I'm crazy, right?

- Craziness comes from turning your back on Love. So, from that perspective, I don't think you're crazy, no.

Averi inhaled sharply and sat back in the deckchair on his veranda. They were both of them wrapped in red blankets on top of their coats and hats and gloves. *This* was perhaps crazy, sitting out in the cold at dawn, watching the mist reluctantly unsheathe itself. But it was beautiful, stark and fresh of all interpretation. Averi smiled at Nyx and watched as she wrapped her fat mittens around her mug of coffee and lifted it to her mouth. She smiled back and drank.

- Do they have names?

- Yeah.

- Are they a secret?

- Clearly nothing is a secret from you.

- Well, I'm not going to broadcast it, if that's what you're worried about.

- Worried? God, I'm talking to you about fictional characters who I speak to, or who rather speak to each other through me. Nothing to worry about there!

- Who says they're any more fictional than you are?

Averi swallowed hard and stared.

- I know, said Nyx. Now you're wondering if you oughtn't to be worried about me.

Averi truly had no idea what he thought. All he could do was puff out his cheeks and empty his lungs.

- Waldo and Hap. Those are their names.

- Waldo and Hap.

- Uh huh.

- Any differentiating characteristics?

- Nope.

- None at all?

- Well, there probably are, but I haven't sussed them out yet.

- So, what do they talk about?

- Well, it's kinda weird, 'cos I've only just started tuning in to them.

- I thought you said you've known them since you were three.

- Sure. But, it's only now that I'm really *aware* of them as they speak. Like – I don't know – imagine you know that your legs walk every day. You don't need anyone to tell you that, but nor do you exactly think about it. They walk but you don't pay any attention to them. Then one day it's as if you tune in to that walking. You suddenly discover that you *are* the legs, you are the movement, and you're even the watcher of the movement. That's what it's like now with Waldo and Hap. I've started to tune in to their movement and it's only 'cos of that that I'm starting to hear what they say.

Nyx was smiling so broadly that Averi was embarrassed.

- Go ahead, laugh!

- I'm not laughing, Averi. Quite the opposite. I know you don't see the perfection of it yet. But trust me; those characters are bringing you home.

- Home to where?

- To who you really are.

Averi made a noise through his teeth. All of a sudden he felt a flood of irritation. He looked out to the sloping lawn as if hoping that would appease him. It was covered in fallen leaves. Another job left undone. If he didn't clear them the grass would soon be a brown mulch. The prunus needed cutting back as well. It was growing absurdly out of control, its red leaves an angry swelling against the mist. Everything was out of control and falling apart, everything.

- Can you give me an idea of what they talk about?

- I don't feel like it right now.

Nyx nodded and sipped her coffee.

Averi watched her out of the corner of his eye. He hated it that she sometimes said things that made him want to burst, and he hated it even more that it made him sound spoiled and ungrateful. He bit the inside of his cheek and pulled the blanket tighter across his chest.

- I am – you know – grateful.
- For what?
- For hanging out.
- I'm not interested in being sociable, Averi.

She was doing it again. It was so infuriating!

- You look shocked.
- Well, what the heck *are* you interested in, then?
- What do you think is happening here?
- Nothing!
- Well, that's truer than you know right now. But, relatively speaking?
- What do you mean?
- Come on, Averi. It's been nine days. You think I sit with you just to shoot the breeze?
- Of course not.
- So, why then?

Nyx was not angry, but she was not smiling either. Averi frowned.

- If you had one question to ask before you die what would it be?

Averi shook his head.

- He who has already faced death – you have one more hour until you die and one question granted.

Averi shrugged and sighed.

- I don't know, what's it all about, I guess.
- That's it?
- Yeah. Like, what the hell is this thing, this me?

- Averi, do you not see the beauty of this timing? The answer to your question, is that not precisely what you saw in that second before blackout?

Averi held himself tight.

- I don't know what I saw.

- Yes, you do. Averi, you are being presented with an opportunity to really find out what's true, to discover without doubt *who you are*. Do you know how rare this is? Something extraordinary is occurring within you. Some profound shift of seeing has taken place: that which you described the night before the storm and then during the storm. Do you imagine life can continue in the same vein after such insight? Do you not see the divine opportunity to investigate what is being revealed to you? This is why I sit with you, why I thought you wished me to sit with you, so that we might unravel this sweet discovery together. I know that you're afraid. It is only natural you should be afraid, for what is being asked of you but to throw every last idea about yourself into the fire of enquiry. And that takes courage. But you don't have to do it alone. I am here to walk this path with you, if you wish, and to see that not a stone is left unturned.

Tears had come and Averi wiped them away, angrily.

- Are we together?

Averi shook his head and laughed at the absurdity of it all.

- But none of what you say makes any sense.

- I know.

- I don't even know what needs enquiry.

- I know, so let's keep it simple. Let's start with Hap and Waldo. They made their appearance today, so let's follow their lead. Who is this one who converses as Hap and Waldo? Can you identify this one?

Averi sniffed, wiped his nose on the back of his sleeve and squinted in Nyx's direction.

- What do you mean? It's me, I guess.

- Be more specific.

- Well, Averi, of course.

- Hmm.

Nyx drank some more. She nodded, but did not look convinced. She turned her head to the mist. Averi shivered. It seemed otherworldly, this shroud of the sky. It deadened sound and breathed secrets. As he watched Nyx, Averi opened his mouth for something to say, but—

- Everything that you see, Averi, this entire phenomenal existence, is temporary. That it comes and goes is its only consistent factor. Trees, sea, people, actions, thoughts, memories, feelings, none of these exist without You.

- But that's ridiculous. If I died the world would still exist.

- Your confusion is that you don't know what 'you' are. Without 'you' there is nothing, there *is* no world. Find out what this 'you' is and then tell me if the world exists without you.

Averi chewed the inside of his lip. He felt his innards again like a spool of annoyance, gradually winding itself tight. He threw back the blanket and stepped down off the veranda and onto the grass.

- You speak in such riddles. I don't see how this helps me. Jesus, I feel like a lab rat.

- Why?

- Because! It all feels so experimental. As if you were gonna test some fatal drug on me.

- *Fatal drug*? Geez, that doesn't sound too hopeful. Although, maybe you've got something there. After all, what I'm talking about is fatal to the mind, which is the best remedy it can have.

- See! There you go again. You're talking in riddles, Nyx, and I don't understand.

- Who doesn't understand?

Averi stretched his arms out wide in exasperation.

- *I* don't understand.

- And which aspect of this 'I' do you mean?

- 'Which aspect, which aspect'! I don't know which aspect.

- Where does understanding or lack of understanding take place?

- I don't know. In the mind, I guess.

- In the mind. So let's begin there. We agree that the mind is the place where your thought of not understanding arises. The mind *thinks* that it doesn't understand. Are we together on this?

Averi exhaled hard, held his hands to his woollen head, and sat heavily on the edge of the stoop.

- Sure.

- Sure?

- *Yes*, Averi replied, truculently. The mind *thinks* that it doesn't understand. I get it.

- But do you? Let's go slowly and retrace our steps. Would you agree that the mind is full of thousands of thoughts all jostling for your attention? These thoughts come in all shapes and sizes – angry ones, excited ones, questioning, learning, wondering ones; and feelings, likewise, are so various and so subtle that sometimes we do not even have names for them. Am I right?

- I guess.

- I think you can do more than guess, Averi. Tell me about your mind and how it works.

Averi raised his eyebrows and shrugged.

- I don't know. There's always a ton of thoughts, of ideas. It's a mess in there and pretty damn crowded.

- Uh huh.

- Like I can be thinking one thought and reckon to myself I pretty much know where I am, and the next minute, bam! Another one comes, another six maybe, and then I don't know what the hell's going on.

- It's a monkey!

- Damn right! It's a goddamn monkey mind!

- And how about now? Let's not speak from memory. Tell me a thought right now.

- Well, for one thing, I'm thinking that I'm freezing my ass off on this ice-cold decking.

- What's aware of that?

Averi stopped laughing at himself and turned to Nyx.

- What do you mean?

- Well, you're aware that the body is feeling cold, right? And then a thought confirms that coldness is felt. Awareness has to be there to know about the cold and also to tell me about the thought, does it not? In fact, there could not be either thought or feeling without awareness; otherwise there would be nothing there to know about thought and feeling. You with me?

- No.

Nyx smiled.

- Give me another.

- Another thought?

- Or emotion, right this moment.

- That I'm trying to understand.

- Then let's find out who this 'tryer' is. Because this 'tryer' is sabotaging everything.

Nyx wrapped the blanket tight around her shoulders.

- Let's keep it simple. There are no mental back-flips required here, Averi. This is straightforward common sense. I have a story that might shed some light.

Before she could begin, Averi stood up from the cold decking and wrapped himself again in his blanket. Nyx waited until he was settled in his chair.

- One day, a young boy visited a wise old sage with a question burning in his heart. Please, old man, he said. Can you help me? I wish to know who I am. The old man smiled for some moments before he replied. He then leaned forward and beckoned the young boy close. First, he whispered, you know that you are. In order to ask, who am I, you must first of all know that you are. That is common sense, no? The real question that is troubling you is to know *as what* you are. You understand very well that you are but you feel you have no clue as to what it *is* that you are.

The young boy looked up, wide-eyed, mystified, but utterly trusting the old man's words. All you need to worry about is knowing that you Are, said the sage. Begin with the statement, I Am. Ignore everything else. Let those words resonate deep in your Being. I Am. This intuitive sense of Existence is not taught to you by parents, or by teachers; it is innate to you. Reside there in that sense of simply Being. Forget 'Who am I?' This question keeps you forever seeking and never discovering. We can discover right now, Averi, if you wish. Draw your attention inward to that sense of Existence in you. Eyes open or closed it shall make no difference. You do whatever feels comfortable.

Averi closed his eyes.

- You know that you exist, do you not?

- But do I? Averi interjected, his eyes snapping open. How do I know that?

- Now the mind is trying to be clever. There is no time for surmising. Find out for yourself. I have no interest in you taking my word for it, Averi. All I ask is that you draw your focus inward, to 'I Am'. Swallow those words and see what arises. What is happening?

- I don't know.

- Okay. Is there anything you can say about this sense of Existence?

- I don't know. It's my brain. I don't know what you want me to say.

- Averi, what I want is for you to allow all thoughts, irritations and sensations to come. We are not in the business of eradicating thoughts. Thoughts can come or not come; neither possibility has any effect on *You*. I am asking simply that you draw your focus away from them and hone in on that intuitive sense of Being within you.

Averi's body deepened into the chair. Like a dropping-down into the farthest fathoms of a well—

- Averi, tell me. If there is one 'knowing' that you know beyond anything else, would it not be that you exist?

- Yes. I exist.

- Now, let us explore what exactly you exist as. Can you say anything about this sense of Existence in you?

- I don't know.

- Does it have a shape?

- I don't think so.

- Does it have a form?

- No, not really.

- Does it have a boundary?

- What do you mean?

- Is it limited to the edges of your body?

- Um, I don't know. I can feel my body.

- I am asking you to draw your attention only to that sense of Existence. Is there a point at where it stops? Does it have a limit?

- No, there's no limit. There can't be a limit because …

Averi opened his eyes while Nyx waited.

- Because it doesn't have a form as such. I don't know what it is, it just— I can't describe it 'cos I don't know what it is. It's like …

- Like what?

- Like a nothing-ness, I don't know. Like space.

- What is this 'it' that you describe as being like space?

- A sense of Being.

- When you say 'it', it sounds like you mean an object that you can see. Can you see your sense of Being?

- No.

- Can you touch it?

- No.

- If you can't see it or touch it, is it in any way an object?

- No. There's no form to it. It just is. It's just space.

- So, your own experience tells you that Existence is synonymous with formless space. You know that you exist. And now you are discovering the nature of Existence. So where are *you* in all this?

Averi could not move from Nyx's gaze. How dark were her eyes and yet what light they held. Averi felt his chest contract and a sob shoot out. It was a sob of laughter and of wonder and of release.

- You *are* that, Averi. You are That.

2

〜

A robin was darting between the cracks of the boards. It flicked its beak in and out of one groove, intent upon something. Perhaps a lost crumb or a dead beetle. What little choice there seemed now in this stripped world. Averi threw a chunk of muffin-cake out onto the lawn and the robin, adept at this game, followed its arc and disappeared with it into the bushes.

- But—

- No, no buts. Your but is a phantom here and cannot help you.

Averi and Nyx caught one another's eye and suddenly burst out laughing. The mist having lifted now, their mirth echoed across the slope and bounced off the old maples.

- Forgive me. Words are such toys. I do enjoy playing with them. Remember, they are just signposts, Averi. You must be cautious to follow their guidance, but not to hold them too close. Then you can play. Oh boy, can you play! To your heart's content. But first we must wipe the slate clean of all falsity. And that, at this stage at least, requires some vigilance.

Averi shivered and yawned and rubbed his eyes. His body was tired and becoming stiff with cold.

- Can we walk?

- Sure, we can walk.

At once, Nyx was up, folding her blanket in neat quarters.

- Don't you feel cold?

- Sure, coldness is felt.

- See, there again – Averi took Nyx's hand to help her down off the stoop – you say 'coldness is felt'. Why can't you say, 'I feel cold'?

- I can say, 'I feel cold'. But then I know what this 'I' refers to, and you are just discovering. So, for the sake of clarity, it is better to say that coldness is felt. Okay, we'll come back to that. But first we need to return to what you were telling me about your mind. We called it a monkey. Always jumping about, never settling on anything for too long, continually inconsistent. And it's not so sequential, either. You must have noticed this. One minute you're talking happily about the nature of Reality, the next you're wondering about the results of sport-ball.

- Even you?

- Perhaps not sport-ball, sure. But you get the picture.

Averi laughed.

- Why do we trust something that is so resolutely inconsistent? Yet we give our minds such credit. We never question its veracity. The only truth that the mind might ever utter is that it doesn't understand, for what I am pointing to, the mind quite rightly can never understand. It is beyond the mind, beyond intellectual understanding. Reasoning and rationality shall not help you here.

Averi walked some paces ahead of Nyx along the narrow lane that led out from his gate and away from town. The tarmac was still wet from the mist and dampness lay on the hedgerows.

- I dunno.

- What don't you know?

- This! All that you're saying. Now it just sounds like words to me.

- I told you to swallow them, not try to understand them.

Averi raised his eyebrows and blew out his cheeks.

- I just bumped my head, Nyx. I had a meltdown for a while. It's no big deal.

- Really?

- Yeah, really. Too much is being made of this. I can't have this conversation.

- Five minutes ago you breathed with clear eyes for the first time in your life. For one beautiful moment you dropped everything. And then, sharp as a tack, a 'but' came in and wanted to make sense of it.

- Yeah, Nyx, 'cos it doesn't last.

- What doesn't last?

- That feeling of space. I can't sit comatose in the corner meditating all day.

- Thank goodness for that, for you should be very dull company indeed. We must investigate this, Averi. We can discover together if that sense of spaciousness comes and goes. Are you with me?

Averi crossed the lane and leaned his weight on the gate that opened onto farmer Lyre's field.

- Averi?

- Okay, look. This is the way I see it. I'm sure what you have to say is great and helpful, but I just don't see things the way you do.

- Is that right?

- Well, sure, maybe for a second, it felt kinda nice, but I gotta look at what's *real*, Nyx. At the *real* truth about this whole crazy episode, so that I can get on with my life, you know?

- You mean real truth as opposed to fake truth?

- Very funny.

- Tell me something, Averi. What do you understand by the word 'truth'?

- Come on, Nyx. Let's not split hairs.

- Oh, finding out the meaning of truth is splitting hairs? You want to base your entire understanding of Existence on a word you can't qualify?

- This is ridiculous. If something is true it's true. You know that.

- What qualifies something as true?

Averi shook his head and backed away from the gate.

- Surely, Nyx continued, that it must always be so. No? That which is true does not waver with time or opinion. Truth is not a part-time condition. Truth is that which is permanent. Let's look at this definition and be clear. We have seen that the mind is constantly wavering and changing; that its very nature is *im*permanence. By that estimation, can it be said that the mind is ever truthful? ... Averi?

- I guess not.

- Right. What does not last is impermanent. That which is impermanent is, in an absolute sense, untrue and unreal. This you are confirming with your own eyes. I'm not asking you to imagine anything, Averi.

I'm not asking you to suppose, or create or theorise. Why do you think that doubt and irritation have such a hold on you? Can you not see that by challenging your own mind on the definition of truth you are in fact challenging the truth of your own mind? No wonder it is up in arms. Of course, your mind is angry, impatient and disbelieving. The mind does not want to be told it is fundamentally untrue, for what then? If your mind and all its thoughts, feelings, memories, experiences and wishes are not fundamentally true, then everything you have believed to be true is not. What a right hook, huh? That's going to floor you like nothing else, for if you are not your mind, then who the hell are you?

Averi was struggling to stand still. His lips bit, his stomach burned, his eyes pricked. He walked back to the gate and surveyed the field. There wasn't much to it at this time of year, just a clayey bog of unturned mud. It was more than one field; it was several in fact, running interlocking squares all the way to the next town. For some reason a memory skittered across Averi's mind of himself and Patch no more than ten or eleven, chasing deep trails through the mud, delicious with fear of meeting Lyre's wrath. Averi saw that the memory seemed to appear out of nowhere. That is to say, it was prompted by what the eyes were looking at, and yet was as transient, as ephemeral, as a ghost. At once, that great fathomless dropping was here; that expansive, panoramic view; that very same that he had experienced in his kitchen, at the quay, and during the storm. He saw that senses were here. A dank, metallic smell of earth was perceived, and the damp, salty air. Nyx was walking towards him. He was watching his own seeing; the crunch of her boot on gravel showed him that he was watching his own hearing. She was standing now by his side leaning her elbows on the gate and looking out at Lyre's field.

- Is there anything, she was saying, you can say that *does* last? Is there anything that you can confirm from your own seeing to be real?

- I Am.

- And you are what?

- Space.

- Timeless, boundless, formless Existence; pure, undifferentiated Awareness.

- It feels like I am watching all the senses as they perceive things.

- For example?

- It's like I'm watching as listening happens. Even now, I'm watching speaking happening.

- And you the watcher? What might you be?

- I don't know. It's not anything.

- *It's* not anything? You just said that *you* were the watcher. And you are what?

- Just awareness. I'm just the awareness, which is—

- Which is what?

- Which is me.

- And this me, does it come and go?

- No, it's always here.

- It's always here. Now it becomes clear that without *you*, without Awareness, nothing exists: no world, no universe, no memories, no personal identity, no feelings, no thoughts, no sky, no field. Nothing exists without primary Awareness, and this my beloved Averi, you have discovered as your own essential Self. What a discovery! What a gift Life has thrown at you. Self has called out to Self, and now we can ask with some real possibility of knowing. Does this Self exert any effort to try to understand?

Averi turned his head and met Nyx's eye. But there was no eye at all. In its place was … Averi had not the language to express what was in its place. It was of no place at all. It had no wish, no desire, no doing, no efforting, no trying. He could not say that there was any*thing* happening at all. All he could say was that *it was*. At once, tears came. Averi wondered how on earth he contained such a fountain. And yet they were so beautiful to shed. How clear it shone that there was—

- No effort at all.

His words came out like a hoarse prayer. If all else was utter confusion these words he knew to be true. Nyx was tilting her head across to him and kicking her foot against the first rung of the gate.

- And the tryer, she whispered. What can you say about him now?

Averi caught his throat as he laughed.

- You don't give up, do you?

Nyx was smiling that patient, unbound smile.

- Where does the tryer come from?

- He's a thought in my mind.

- And what sees even the recognition of that?

Averi stopped, and caught Nyx sideways. He sniffed and wiped each eye with the back of his hand.

- Something is there prior to all thoughts, Averi, as we have proved; prior even to thoughts about thoughts.

That cheeky, cosmic glint was shining like mercury.

- Awareness is there, said Averi, nodding his awareness of his own Awareness across the panoramic landscape of home.

It felt like silence beyond any concept of silence. It felt like peace.

- And I am That.

3

~~

A new girl has arrived on Saffron Ward and her name
is Lydia. I say 'girl' because she cannot be more
than nineteen or twenty. Poor thing, she looks about as
splintered as a starved sparrow. She has that plain-waif
look about her that is so popular in magazines these
days. Plain that has become the new beautiful in a rather
haunting way.

Yesterday brought the first whiff of change in the air
when Jude did not show up to breakfast. Mareka was on
duty, but unfortunately Sarah was in one of her more
corrosive moods, and so we didn't get much out of her.

- You know, Mareka, Sarah said. Out of all the idiots
here who pass themselves off as nurses you really are the
worst. Mind you, I bet we get the lowest of the lowest
pickings at this place. It stands to reason, though, if you
think about it. I mean if you had any nous you'd be off
working in paediatrics or as a theatre nurse, really saving
lives. Instead you're in this prison of legalised kidnap,

actually helping to harm and mutilate and torture innocent people out of their minds.

In fact, she had a point. This is hardly an institution of love and recuperation. Poor little Mareka, though. She's about as harmful as a pink daisy.

- Are you finished, she asked, reaching out to take Sarah's bowl.

- Do I look finished? Christ, and now you're trying to starve us.

And she wrapped her elbow around her bowl like children do to stop their friends from copying. Reynardo piped up next.

- Well, I wonder if they let Jude go home.

- Either that or he topped himself.

- Sarah!

- Fat Nandi! she shouted back.

Fat Nandi spun again on his seat to turn his back to Sarah. Nandi is obese. Frankly, it would be rude to ignore it. Unfortunately, Sarah's sobriquet has been set in cement, and now even I have to catch myself. Sarah pushed her grey wiry hair out of her eyes and scooped up the last of her cornflakes, not in the least bit concerned by the slump in Nandi's shoulders. I wondered then, as I often wonder, what led this grizzled, mouse-eyed being through these doors. There is a rumour that she once was a head teacher of a prestigious girls' school. It is hard to see beneath the polka dot leggings and the ragged, woollen jumper that has grown from age; beneath the liver-spotted skin and the red-tarnished cheeks of fury. I wonder if an immensely tight leash was forcibly un-spun and has left her reeling ever since. What miracles they could be unearthing, these doctors, if only they dared to scrape back those layers of rage and discover what exactly comprises a Sarah; or indeed a

Reynardo, or a Rose who must always separate colours into groups, or a silent Jane who must always sit in the corner. Do they even *know* to wonder what led silent Jane into her reverie? What treasures could be uncovered! To think these psychiatrists have such wealth at their fingertips and all they can conjure up is the best dosage of compliance. Fear of the mind is palpable. It breathes distrust and judgement into all proceedings. The arrival of Lydia is the perfect example.

Her first entrance tonight was disturbing, even for us. It was late, around ten, and lights had just gone out. I can only describe it as the high-pitched distress call of an elk. A pin-point screech, bending painfully to a hoarse bark. My God, it was the most devastating suffering I have ever heard. Bedroom lights came on, doors opened, and out we stood in our pyjamas and dressing gowns. A thin creature had somehow crawled its legs almost to the height of the passageway ceiling, while leaning its shoulders on John, the night warden. John is Titan, Gargantua and Goliath all in one, so it was of little consequence to him to have this spindly spider paddle its legs across the wall. He held tight to her arms as she struggled and flailed, and with one neat pull he had her flat to the floor on her belly. She lifted her head and howled that elk's cry, and through the matted tangle of her long hair could be seen blood at her mouth. Quite a good deal in fact; her lips and teeth were running with it. It was enough to drive Rose into a panic. She shoved her fists into her mouth and then *she* started to wail. Jesus, now I really know the meaning of a lunatic asylum. Anastasia bared her fury with much spit and thrust Rose back into her room; meanwhile John was lying almost flat on top of that poor waif. It is a wonder he didn't break her back. But she was fearless. She kicked her legs and pulled at whatever she could catch. Remarkably, it looked as if she were half escaped – perhaps she had dealt him a damaging kick – but before she could lift herself up, a night nurse, who had just come back from his break, came running to help John. And now two grown men were lying flat on the back of a nineteen-year-old girl. Anastasia, roused and terrifying, barked at them to hold Lydia down, which was ludicrous really since she couldn't be more held if they tried. What Anastasia meant was to hold her while she injected a sedative. Lydia saw it coming and begged to be let go. Huge tears were running down her cheeks as she said she was sorry, she was sorry, she is sorry. And at that last apology I am catching her eye. It is grey and dispossessed. Where have we come to that we must replace love with barbiturates? I feel my legs walk forward now and my arms reach out to this child. A voice, Anastasia's, is on full volume to warn me, but my attention is on Lydia. I feel myself kneel. Her body has softened and the men are pulling her to her feet.

- Please John and, forgive me, I don't know your name, I say to the other guy. Please let her go. Can't you see how frightened she is?

Perhaps it is the softness of my voice, for the two men falter. Anastasia is ready to burst. Her fingers grab my arms. They have bruised me before, these fingers, but I am not deterred. She is only afraid of what she cannot control.

- Anastasia, I say. I understand.

I do understand. To see such horror in another human being is to imagine such horror in oneself. So walls are built, and most shall last a lifetime.

Anastasia has crouched behind my back, her formidable bulk pressing as she tries to lift me off the floor. I don't know if I have suddenly gained fifty pounds but lift me she cannot. Somehow I manage to slide forward and pull Lydia into my arms. She is soft as putty now, but shaking like a rattle of bones. Her wide eyes are far too large and vulnerable for such a small frame. She reaches like an infant, wraps herself around my neck and I stroke her hair away from the blood.

- Reynardo! I call out.

Bless him, he knows at once. Reynardo is a stickler for clean handkerchiefs in his pockets. He stumbles forward and produces a neatly folded square of red checkers. He squeezes his arm in between the blockade of Anastasia, the Titan and the night nurse, and I am able to clean away the mess of tears, blood and snot. I think at this point I am being threatened with the loss of privileges. I don't like to stoke the fire by adding that I have none to lose. What matters is letting Lydia know she is not alone.

I wish for a moment I had a camera on this scene: patients hovering in the corridor; Rose out of her room again in her pink woollen dressing gown, whimpering on her knuckles; Sarah trying to spark a mutiny; Fat Nandi, wobbling from one fat leg to another; silent Jane poking her head out of her bedroom door, blank as a wall; Reynardo crouched down and offering words of support to both Lydia and his Lili; and the blockade moving as one body in a veritable push-me-pull-you across the floor. Perhaps we tussle for hours. I really don't know. I do know that in her fear Lydia has wet herself. The night nurse jumps back in disgust, and Anastasia curses under her breath. She shouts at John to fetch the bucket and mop, and disappears herself for a cloth.

I don't mind. Lydia and I sit together and rock in her mess. This little one has broken her wings and Saffron shall not be the place to mend them.

4

How uncanny that our little sparrow can sing. Such Celtic ballads as curl your heart. We have been asked not to encourage her. I understand that her timing is not always— Well, let us just say there are times when we would all rather sleep. It seems to me, however, that punishing her will not break her out of her isolation, but rather provoke it. I have discovered that by lying on the bed next to her and stroking her hair, she gradually lowers the volume, until she is so lulled by her own song that she eventually drops to sleep. It is extraordinary that she allows me this close when, even after a week, she has not so much as asked me my name. One slight move and she whimpers, and so it means that for the moment I must sleep alongside her. Anastasia refused at first, but Dmitri was sympathetic. He has such a gentle demeanour, our lovely Russian. He leaned his head around Lydia's bedroom door the other night and put his finger to his lips.

- I shall not tell, he whispered, in his thick lilt, and he winked as he carefully shut her door.

Moments of kindness are so rare these days. Even now when I think of it, it makes me want to cry.

- Have you returned to silence?

- Silence is not a place I return to. Silence is what I am.

I have started off on the wrong foot. Katherine is biting the inside of her cheek. She missed the last session and no one else even turned up in her place. She apologised when she arrived today, but she has not yet explained her absence. It sits there between us like a set of crossroads. I have the impression that Katherine has not yet made up her mind which path she wants to take.

- I'm sorry, I add. I was thinking of Lydia.

- Your new protégée.

Doctor Kolinsky doesn't say this unkindly, but nonetheless I am shocked.

- First Bill, now Lydia.

- You say that as if Reynardo had been dropped.

- Hasn't he?

I am honestly so stunned that it takes me a few moments to really sit and think about this. Is this how my actions are perceived? For if that is the case then I must look and see if what she says is true.

- You see a tendency, do you not, Katherine continues, to rush in as the rescuer and express by deed, if not word, clear disdain of medical expertise. Do you think you know better than the doctors, Lili?

I look up to see if there is sarcasm in the use of that name. But I cannot see any. Katherine's eyes are clear and straightforward; I might even say *concerned*.

- Reynardo is not in the least bit dropped. In fact, he has been spending time with both Lydia and I. His needs are different, surely you can see that. Lydia is new here and is more demanding right now. Naturally, for the moment some extra effort is given her way. I'm concerned about her reaction to the depot. I know you're not her consultant, but Doctor Wood pays no attention to her complaint. Perhaps you haven't seen a patient when the dose kicks in; otherwise you might be concerned too. She slurs her words, she dribbles like an infant, and she becomes so lethargic she looks like a vegetable. This says nothing about the pain in the joints and the acute anxiety. All of this I can vouch for, as you know. As for my tendency, as you call it, to feel another's pain and hold them through it, well, I can imagine worse tendencies. I'm sorry if that comes across as arrogance. I see that it must.

Katherine is turning the ring on her index finger. She has not taken my file out of her bag today, though it stands upright, on show as a reminder.

- You think you can feel someone else's pain?

- I don't think that I can; I know that I can.

The minute the words escape, it's clear how they're received. I try to find a way to explain.

- Thinking has nothing to do with intuiting. In fact, thinking only gets you into trouble and builds unnecessary stories. I've learned the hard way with that one.

- Do you mean to say that you have some sort of *psychic* ability?

I know I shouldn't, but a laugh comes out. I know where we are going with this: pathology and symptoms. Another dead end.

- Am I psychic? That's one of those unnecessary stories and a very loaded label. But if you mean does listening happen, then yes, I guess it does.

- Here we have it again. You have dissociated yourself, Lili. Listening happens, you say. Not, *I* listen. I think we should try and understand why.

From my angle of sitting, Katherine is half in shadow. I have to squint slightly at the light. There is such a warm stream coming in through the mesh that it's possible to imagine a summer's day. Thoughts come as they do on a film strip. Summer images: the lake on the heath, lying on a picnic blanket and reading in the sun, walking barefoot in my grandparents' garden. I'm sure that if I told Katherine, she would think I was longing for them. I stand at that moment and walk to the mesh. By laying my left cheek flat to the metal and looking right-ways I can just about make out the great oak that lies on the opposite side of the fence in the park. It is strange that it used to be my favourite park and that I used to walk past that great oak every day. It is strange that all of a sudden Katherine is beginning to sound like an actual psychiatrist. Admittedly, my former silence must have been something of a stumbling block. But I have seen dozens of consultants over these months; I have witnessed interactions between other patients and psychiatrists. This is the first time that *real* questioning, *real* interest has ever taken place. I wonder what has changed. Perhaps me; perhaps my own readiness to speak has unlocked her curiosity. It is as if our last session was Pandora's key. At this stage, though, I want to know if it is mere curiosity. There is little point in us continuing if I am to be simply dissected into scientific boxes.

- You know there is nothing we want more, Lili, than for you to leave.

She has turned her head at a sharp angle to be able to look me in the eye. The sun has caught her now and, from this higher perspective, I see that she has light freckles across her nose. For a moment she looks as innocent and as untouched as a child.

- Have you heard the aphorism, 'Know thy Self'?

Katherine pauses as if wary of a catch.

- Of course.

- Most people consider themselves free, Katherine, and that I, being in here, am not. Freedom is our most prized possession; we consider it our most basic right. So much so we are ready to fight to the death for it, and yet we have not the faintest idea what this freedom is. To you I can never be free so long as I am locked in here. I do not long to leave as you think I do; I do not consider myself trapped as you think I do. Thoughts come about both, make no mistake, but they do not concern the Freedom that I am. To know the Self is to know Freedom. It *is* Freedom.

- Is that not the possibility here? To understand yourself?

- You think I mean my personality.

- Well, fascinating as it may be, Katherine replies with impatience, I hardly think investigating Reynardo's, or Lydia's, or my personality shall bring you any closer to understanding yours.

Suddenly, and quite unexpectedly, anger shoots through and spins me across the room. I end up somewhere near the door. My head bangs against the wall, not on purpose, but from sheer momentum.

- Lili?

- We can play this game if you wish, Katherine, but truly it shall get us nowhere; not that there is – *truly* – anywhere to go.

- What game?

- This game! The 'concept' game. But it shall lead us up a blind alley at every turn.

- It seems to me that it is you who are playing the game, Katherine shouts. You speak in riddles that are impossible to understand.

Yes, I see that. Dear God, I do see it. Urgent tears are suddenly falling. I don't know if it is the arrival of Lydia and her deluded suffering or those eager cornflowers looking up at me, but something has turned the wrench on this dial: something that wills me to speak, despite another voice, which urges caution.

- Dear God, help me explain. It is not up to me to impress where someone is not ready. And yet if ever there were a relative trap then this is it. Fail to explain and here I remain. I beg of You to tell me if this is really what is required. Clear me of all arrogance. Let only Truth pass these lips. Dear God, whatever smacks of this mind and its manipulations, may You dissolve it in Love—

I feel my body slide down the wall and my head drop into my hands. Each syllable of that prayer is a lock on the door of this place. Doctor Katherine Kolinsky is staring at me as if I had just told her the moon was purple. There is no putting the cat back in the bag now. There is nothing to do but hope that tiny fluttering heart will hand itself over.

She is back in shadow and I feel her fear curling at the edges.

- I know you're afraid.

- Afraid of what, she asks.

- Of this. Of the potential here. These questions are an earthquake, Katherine. Trust me, they shall swallow you whole and break the one you think is you into pieces.

- What questions?

- Who is this 'I' that you imagine I dissociate from?

- I don't—

- I know you don't. You don't have to understand, Katherine. And trust me, I am not trying to be deliberately obtuse. Our first step on this journey is to accept that we are all each other's teachers.

- You consider yourself my teacher?

- No more than you are mine. It seems incongruous that I should try to explain when there appears, at least on the surface, to be no questioning in you. And yet, this is the learning. So many beings are desperately asking questions without even knowing that they are. They sense the confusion, they are confused; but they have not the faintest notion what they are confused about. Is this beginning to make any sense?

Katherine has begun to breathe high up in her chest.

- Life has thrown us together, don't you see that?

- It's very comforting to believe that—

- And clearly there is some learning we have for each other. All this scientific apathy – it reeks of laziness and fear.

Katherine opens her mouth as if to speak, but nothing comes out. Instead, that shaft of sunlight shuts in on itself. We are back to grey walls and grey table. The waif-bird is singing, an ancient, fractured song. We let it sit in the air, its high treble bemoaning some loss. If only she knew that nothing was lost. My mind, too, loves this 'tragedy', sculpts all manner of meaning, bathes in that melancholic psalm and finds such beauty in woe. Holy moly! What a drama! There is no woe, only that which we imagine. For now, this psychiatrist is as terrified as that sparrow, both locked in the prison of their minds. The real beauty, oh Katherine, if you realised ... well, what to say ...? If you realised, there would be nothing left to say.

5

⌘

‑Lili?

- Yes, Reynardo?

- Kolinsky says we can go for a walk.

- *What?*

Reynardo is already buttoned into his duffle coat. His blue striped scarf and green woollen hat look about as pert and excited as he is.

- Well, give me a bit of warning, why don't you! Geez!

And Reynardo giggles.

- How long have we got?

- Two hours. Two-thirty to four-thirty.

- Reynardo! It's two-forty now! Honestly, you are a pickle. Help me get my coat, then.

I make believe at being cross, which only makes Reynardo giggle more. He holds up my black anorak and we struggle with an inside-out arm, pulling and pushing and tugging and turning, until we are both laughing like children.

- How much money do we have?

Reynardo turns out his pockets onto my bed: a clean, folded handkerchief, a worn-out eraser, one chewed pen lid, a couple of fruit drops and some empty wrappers, two fifty-pence pieces, a twenty-pence piece and about a dozen filthy coppers.

- Okay. And I do the same.

It's hardly much better. Three pound coins, thank goodness, and a couple of twenties.

- It's the Ritz for tea, then.

- Can I take you, Lili?

- You certainly may, and I hold out my arm. I should be delighted, sir.

Since we are the first walkers in several months everyone turns to look. We are a couple of celebrities for two fat minutes. Rose comes out of her room to watch; Greg, our handsome musician, whoops and beats the air.

- Go, Lili! Go, Reynardo!

Sarah looks up from her armchair with as little turning of her body as possible. She scowls and turns back to the television. Fat Nandi pulls me by the arm and whispers tightly in my ear.

- Lili, post this could you?

Fat Nandi thrusts a letter without a stamp on it into my hand. I know he sends letters to his wife each week but that she never responds. Given the lack of stamps, I begin to wonder now if it is because she never receives them.

- Of course, Nandi, and I pat his arm to reassure him.

This shall seriously dent our coffee fund, but I haven't the heart to say no. I catch sight of Lydia leaning at the nurses' desk. Her expression is, as always, inscrutable. I cannot help but feel a moment of guilt at leaving her. The guilt is not real, however, and I know that everything is as it should be. I smile and she turns away.

Just as we reach the door, Mareka runs after us and whispers in my ear that if we make it back by four-forty-five at the latest, she shall not tell. She's such a poppet. But I don't know who she thinks she is going to tell. She is the one on duty! She keys in the security code and we are out.

It is only five minutes' walk to the entrance of the park. It seems strange that it is not encouraged; to come here, that is. Surely even supervised daily walks would at the very least clear the nostrils of that stuffy, wretched odour of a ward. No amount of sanitiser spray can do it. How delicious is this air, crisp and untrammelled. Boy, I can feel each pore inhale. I had not imagined my senses were so raw.

Reynardo is kicking his feet up and spraying the lawns with dried leaves. The gardeners shan't be pleased, but who am I to destroy his fun? Russet and coffee and tangy orange; a kaleidoscope of autumn endings. He looks so sweet, sixty-four years of condensed joy, though perhaps the doctors wouldn't see it that way.

There is a shilly-shallying of paths in this park, and the great tease each time is to know which one to take. My personal favourite is the 'avenue'. It runs along the western edge, a tunnel that always changes. In spring and summer it is the laburnum of all smiles. How I love that celebration, as it secretly enfolds us, whispering of long-lost days and trailing gowns. See how my mind loves a story! Quite deliriously, and I make no bones about it. In autumn and winter the avenue is a stark shell, but secret nonetheless, guiding us up out of the rabbit hole and over to the lake where, even today, there are boys sailing boats. We might have stepped back an era or two were it not for the modern pushchairs and a ringing phone.

- Lili, come!

Reynardo is on his knees at the edge of the water, pointing a stick and leaning perilously close.

- I can catch it if you hold my arm.

- Reynardo, you're too heavy—

But unless we are both to fall in I have to pull with all my weight so that Reynardo might reach the capsized boat. There is no stopping a determined fox. The little owner of the boat is shouting.

- You've got it, nearly; he's nearly got it, Mum.

- Whoa! Another inch and she was a goner!

Reynardo beams at his catch – a lovely blue and white hull and pristine white sails – turning it around with an artist's eye.

- There you go, young man.

The mother smiles and thanks us, and reminds her son to do the same. She looks at me, and then to the fox, and I see her appraise his coat and his hat and his child-like enthusiasm. This man was once a highly respected lighting designer for theatre and opera. Winchester, Cambridge, all the trimmings, until breakdown came at forty-five and drove him out of his life. This woman shall never guess at that; how could she? Instead, she shall nod and quickly make her exit, pulling her little boy close. There is no judgement here; only an acknowledgement that we incite more fear than fear itself.

On the other side of the lake is the café with its awning and the tables and chairs. Reynardo has chosen his seat and is ready with his cigarette pouch.

- What'll we have, he says.

- Well, give us your change, then. I laugh.

And he throws down his coins, retrieving the fruit drop.

- D'you think we've got enough for a doughnut?

I love this place. It's simple, a little rough around the edges, with the view of the lake and the sloping terrace. In the end I had enough for two cappuccinos and a custard tart. I cut it fairly in two halves and Reynardo supervised with the precision of a draughtsman. Now we sit in comfortable silence, warm in our bellies and sweetened in tooth. Reynardo is rolling a cigarette. He does it so exactly, so beautifully, it almost looks delicious to smoke. I turn my head to look through the café door and to the clock on the wall behind the counter. Four-twenty. What a lovely afternoon. Made even more perfect now that I shall not mind when it is over.

- Reynardo? What is your most favourite thing in the world?

- Sitting here with you, Lili.

He says it so precisely, so unselfconsciously, that my mouth drops open in surprise. Reynardo lights his cigarette from the yellow lighter he has borrowed from the café and takes a deep inhale. For some moments I am speechless. In fact, if I try to talk I shall cry. Here it is: a whisper of that which I speak. He does not look to any imagined future. Such things do not exist for Reynardo. His is an innocence without expectation. How beautiful. If only he were able to recognise himself.

For then he could drop this play. As it is he carries a world of back story in those duffle pockets. It seems a paradox that some shift has broken through to child-like freedom, while the mind's fear keeps the fox on stage. How to explain this? It is a mystery, and yet so clear as to puncture all doubt.

Reynardo looks at his watch. He folds his pouch into his pocket, conceals the prized lighter, and stands up. He walks around to my chair, humming something familiar. He pulls out my chair, helps me to my feet, and slides his arm through mine. The words of his song betray that it may take more than one lifetime to unravel this sweet being.

> *'A song of love is a sad song*
> *Hi-lili Hi-lili Hi-lo'*

But who am I to break his bubble? It is his protection for now, and for that I see its beauty. I imagine mentioning to Katherine the idea of many lifetimes. I don't think I'd be enjoying many more walks after that conversation. The thought makes me smile and join Reynardo in song. It doesn't matter that, as we walk by, people laugh at our voices raised to the sky. For neither of us has the slightest inclination to stop.

> *'Hi-lili Hi-lili Hi-lo Hi-lo*
> *Hi-lili Hi-lili … Hi-lo'*

6

᷍᷍᷍

—**W**hat's up? You look sad.

- I do?
- Uh huh.

Nyx stood straight, leaned backwards, and stretched her spine. She and Averi had been collecting peeler crab since dawn. It was still early enough to have the beach to themselves. Only mad fisher-folk would consider rising this early to wade into rock pools for fish bait in a cold winter wind. They had come to the northern-most beach of the island. Its rugged dunes ran for five miles along this shore: fine white sand, a sea like a flat-top of marble and a sky like mother-of-pearl. The best finds were higher up the tide at the farthest rocky outcrop. Here at the half-mark they were plentiful and easy to distinguish.

Averi pulled away the end section of one of the crab's legs. Sure enough the outer hard shell peeled off to reveal the soft replacement. It seemed rather pretty with its mottled green shell. Why should the poor fellow be removed from his homely rock pool? It wasn't his fault that the waves had thought fit to deposit him halfway up the beach. Now that he was here, surely he had as much right to scuttle under rocks as anyone. Averi threw the peeler into the bucket. Crab autonomy to fisherman's bait in three easy seconds. What was fair about that? Averi leaned hard on his waders and pushed himself up.

- Have you ever fished? Ever once in your life?

Nyx smiled.

- Not in water.

- Well, I'd sure like to see the kind of fish *you're* catching. You even eat the stuff?

- You know I don't.

- I don't get it.

Clearly they had had this conversation before. Nyx took off her gloves, sat on a rock a few metres away and undid her rucksack.

- You hungry?

- So wait, I just wanna be clear on this.

- Okay. Nyx laughed, taking out a flask and unscrewing the top.

- So, you run a store for fishermen and you even come out here and mess around for peelers and mussels.

- Don't forget my white ragworms.

- Which essentially means setting these guys up to be killed to attract another bunch of suckers also to be killed. And you, with the way that you talk, I don't know, you sound like you believe that life is sanctified, or something.

- Did I ever tell you that I was state worm charmer?

Steam rose as Nyx poured hot black coffee into the first mug.

- *Isn't that what you believe?*

- I don't believe in anything, Averi. I told you that. You want some coffee?

And she held out the mug for Averi to take. Averi took no notice of the mug. He was too busy pacing between rocks.

- How can you not believe in anything? It doesn't make sense.

Averi grabbed a bucket to show its contents.

- So, how about these guys?

- We fish for as much as we need on this island, Nyx replied. No more, no less. I see no difficulty in that. What do you see, Averi? Tell me why you look so sad.

Averi smiled, bitterly.

- And we're back to me.

- I guess we will keep coming back to you until there is no one left to come back to.

Averi turned and stared, apoplectic.

- You wanna know what I see, Nyx? I'll tell you what I see. That these guys need to be free.

And he tipped the contents upside down into the closest pool and threw the bucket across the sand as hard as he possibly could.

- You know what else?

Nyx was staring without answering.

- I see someone who feels so damn responsible all the time, and I hate it. I hate that I don't understand what's happening to me. I see this snivelling, pathetic non-person who doesn't even know who he is anymore. And worse than all of that I see a complainer; a self-obsessed, self-indulgent whiner, whose very breath reeks of negativity. That's what I see!

And he sat down heavily with his back to Nyx. Averi knew it was a childish gesture, but somehow he couldn't stop himself.

Nyx was pouring cream from a second flask into her mug.

- Have you so quickly forgotten your deeper seeing?

Of course he hadn't forgotten. But Averi felt too … too … *God*, Averi no longer knew what he felt. Only that as a result of … *that* … nothing made sense any more. And now this, his life of the sea, the only thing he had ever been sure about and known so intimately that his own fibres breathed its rhythm. This had been all he'd known, all that his grandfather had known, and his father … Averi dropped his head into his hands.

- Patch came to see me last night. He wants me back on the *Chariot*. They all do. They're asking for me, Nyx, don't you see that? What am I supposed to tell them? That I'm going crazy, that I'm going out of my mind? That I hate the *Chariot* and all she does? That I never want to set foot on her again? God, Nyx, that's turning my back on everything. And he saw it. Nyx, Patch saw. His little face, it broke my heart to see it. I can't talk to them, don't you get it? Trindar and his goddamn beautiful silence. I can't look at him. Raul can't even raise a voice to me anymore, and Haiti looks at me like …

- Like what?

- Like I'm some sort of lost soul, that's what. I love 'em, I do, but I can't be with them right now. I just don't know what to say. They look so goddamn hurt.

Averi sprung up again. There was suddenly so much to say.

- And it's not just the boys.

- Who else?

- Everyone, for Chrissakes! Everyone looks at me like I'm broken or something.

- Is that so bad?

- I can't bear to walk into Quartermaine. They all stop and stare at the walking tragedy. And the minute I actually lock eyes they freak out.

- Why do you think that is?

- I don't know! If I knew that, *I* wouldn't be so freaked out! It's that look.

- What look?

- That look that says, what the hell are you doing with your life?

- And that concerns you why?

Averi laughed and opened his arms wide as if to survey his surroundings.

- Geez, isn't it obvious?

- Not especially.

Averi shook his head disbelievingly.

- It concerns you because you believe the same thought into existence.

Again, the heat of anger was welling. Averi pulled off his hat as the heat rose into his face. He could not even bear to look at Nyx.

- The thought arises most persistently that you should and *need* to know what to do with your life.

- I'm thirty-four years' old and the furthest I've been from this island is five miles out to sea.

- You don't need to leave your backyard to find out who you are. But this thought, this most tenacious of thoughts is believed. Who *is* this one who thinks he must know what to do with his life? Whose life are you talking about? You have the audacity to think that you ought to know what to do with life when you don't even know the one who is supposedly living it. Seems a little mixed up to me.

Averi snorted impatience.

- I know that you're angry. And it's good that you are.

- I don't even know what I'm angry at!

- That's even better. Now we can really scrape things clean.

- God, Nyx. I don't know why the hell I trust *you*. I must be out of my mind.

- Now we're getting somewhere.

Averi caught Nyx's eye, not quite long enough to really meet her, but long enough to make them both smile. It was true he had not the faintest idea what he was angry at. And yet there it was: a boulder that seemed to shut off all exits. He looked at Nyx, then looked away; looked at Nyx again and then looked away once more. What on earth drew him to this woman? The obvious was obvious. Anyone could see that she was beautiful. Yet it wasn't that. He couldn't quite put his finger on what it was. Something inexplicable that was both terrifying and a comfort. He thought of his boys, his childhood friends, how together they had been through all times, on land and off land, in all weathers, in all conditions; how each facet drew them closer, and how each character was borne by the others; how Patch owed everything to his wide-eyed innocence and endless sanguinity; how Trindar sat deep inside himself but never failed in his silent support; how Haiti sang his resilient determination; and how Raul harangued, rebuked, disagreed and criticised. No storm was ever mounted without them. But this last one was different. Somehow Averi had sailed into new territory. This was entirely unchartered. He knew as little of these depths as of the Milky Way. He had not even a compass. His only certainty was that he could not take those boys with him. Not this time. It broke him to know it. Never had he felt more at sea than on this patch of rocky certainty. And once again they came. If he had not been so exhausted, Averi would have laughed at the clockwork regularity of his tears.

7

~Do you know where I should like to begin?

Averi raised his eyebrows. He bit down on his ham and cheese sandwich and grinned. Salt tears, salt spray and metallic coffee. He didn't understand why it all tasted so good. And if there was one thing he understood about Nyx, it was that her beginnings were never really beginnings.

- I know what you're gonna say.

- You do, huh?

- Yeah, said Averi, wiping his mouth with the back of his hand. Something about finding out about the one who I *think* I am.

Nyx smiled.

- So, you have been listening. Actually, I want to return to the one who thinks he's responsible. Let's identify him, first of all.

Averi watched as Nyx folded her empty sandwich wrapper into quarters, stored it away in the pocket of her rucksack and wiped her knees of crumbs. It was astonishing to Averi that she managed not only to remember all manner of details about things he had said during any one conversation, but that she could also select at will from countless of their conversations, as if she were filing through a box of index cards.

- Tell me about that one. Responsible for what?

- I don't know, really. I guess I feel responsible for how other people feel; the boys, for example. I suppose you wanna know where that comes from.

- Not especially, but we can go there if you'd like to. … You look confused.

- Well, yeah. Isn't that what you people do? Trawl through reasons for why we do things?

- Averi, we are perhaps trying to run before we can walk. But what I can say to you is this. Know your story, don't believe in it. I'm going to express something to you now that I don't want you to try and understand. *I see everything with detached intimacy*. What can such testimony mean? I *see* the personality, but I *am not* the personality. Personality appears within Me. From this perspective, from the freedom of Self, the idiosyncrasy and the detailed learning of this individual called Nyx is seen. The detail makes her female and with all the physical characteristics that you see. The traits, the likes and dislikes, the foibles and tendencies are all a part of this character called Nyx. All are part of an apparent story that has the potential to bring the realisation that this character is only a temporary appearance within permanent Awareness. Many traditions have spoken of 'annihilating the ego'. Perhaps you have heard of this. While the core of this sentiment is true, it misses one vital component: that the ego is in fact the path to knowing that which lies beyond ego. What a paradox!

- But, Nyx—

- I know it sounds confusing. But let me just finish. It is better that I speak and risk confusion so that we can lay it all on the table and then work our way towards understanding. A more intelligent expression might be 'to annihilate the *conditioned* mind', and yet still, and this is the crux, that very conditioning is our guide home. I know, language can be tricky, so let us peel back one layer at a time. First of all, what is even meant by conditioning? Does that word make any sense to you?

- I'm not sure.

- To be conditioned is to be taught to believe – to be indoctrinated into believing – a certain way about something. This is not as sinister as it sounds. It is precisely what occurs for each and every one of us. From the moment of your birth, from the moment you were named Averi, conditioning began in both home and society. It happens unavoidably, unconsciously, dependent for its flavour upon the era we are born into and the prevailing social mores. Even the political structure of our society and our roles as males and females within a particular society all shape our idea of ourselves. And then of course comes the more personal conditioning that takes place at home: the specific relations between us and our parents, our siblings and our friends; their personalities and their own conditioning coming up against what we have learned. Our parents condition us even by loving us; our teachers condition us a little more consciously perhaps, and yet still, they too are determined by their own conditioning about who they think they are. It is subtle and broad, both at the same time. From this perspective there can be no judgement about a conditioned mind; it is part of what it is to be human. But there is no doubt that it causes havoc. We'll get to the havoc in a minute, but first tell me about yours.

- Mine?

Averi pulled his hat back down over his ears and squinted.

- Yes, tell me, what does it mean to be an 'Averi'?

Averi laughed; it seemed such a ludicrous question.

- Well—

- Where was he born?

- Here on this island. Never left.

- Without comments, tell me.

Averi took a breath and chewed the inside of his lip. He knew where Nyx was going.

- Mother left when I was six, never saw her again. Father had a breakdown, never really recovered. Now in a home with dementia.

- Okay, those are the broad strokes. But within those happenings are myriad distinctions; myriad subtle emotions that formed the relationship between you and your mother when she was present and you and the mother who left; between the father before and the father bereft. All of which have formed your idea about yourself and have given you a clear sense of identity. And this is aside from your relationship with this island, with the boys, with the sea; aside from the relationship with yourself. There are certain traits that you have been born with; some you have developed and honed as a result of your conditioning; others were given to you for this lifetime as a backdrop to learning; as this one's map for Awareness. Okay, let me put it this way.

Let us say, for the sake of argument, that the mother leaving the son at such a young age creates in the child many conflicting emotions. Naturally, the most obvious is the pain of abandonment. Next come self-blame, anger, yearning, confusion, resentment, idealising, until the child has a complete self-image mirrored through the pain of abandonment. Needless to say, unless fully faced and understood, all future relationships – particularly with women – shall be unconsciously tarred with this learned identity.

Now, when I said I wasn't especially interested in finding out why you behave in the way that you do, the reason was not because it is not important. On the contrary, these aspects of the personality *must* be faced. There is no choice here. They must be brought under the microscope so that each subtlety may be seen in sharp focus. But this is not my job; this is not why I am talking to you. I am not a therapist. I do not have time to pick through the material details, and nor would my conclusions be necessarily relevant. That must be left to your own wisdom. What I am pointing to is that these details are the key to recognising that you are *beyond* the detail; because by pressing those buttons, by having to jump into the fire of our own story, we may somehow be squeezed dry of all identification with that story. I know this may sound complicated, Averi. But truly, when seen, it is so simple, and as obvious as that eyes give sight. The 'you' that you understand as the personality is but an aspect within the Impersonal 'You'.

- But how can I as a person be impersonal? It doesn't make sense.

- Of course, to be a person is entirely personal, Averi. But what is being pointed to here? To that which lies prior to the person, to that which is *Im*personal.

- Nyx, I—

- What?

- It all just sounds like pretty words to me. I'm sure you're right, and I'm happy to take your word for it; but like I said before, I can't always see what you see.

- Okay. First of all, I don't want you ever to take my word for it. This has to be your direct experience, not supposition. That *is* just words. Averi we couldn't be having this conversation unless you had already had a taste of what I am talking about.

Averi lifted his head.

- In your kitchen that night, on the quay and on board the *Chariot*. Some profound shift of perspective occurred within you. This knowing is unravelling itself in you as we speak; only the mind is afraid. It is quite honestly so terrified that at this point it would rather bury all intuition and remain in ignorance than face the clarity of truth. But that way lies madness, Averi. To turn your back on Love, on intuitive knowing, on the godly principle within you is the path to insanity and suffering. You have a stark choice, Averi, if there is truly any choice at all. I am here for this purpose and this purpose alone: to prick the bubble of delusion once and for all. This needle is sharp, Averi, and takes no prisoners.

Averi laughed and wiped his eyes with the back of his hand. A great well of emotion had suddenly unleashed itself at Nyx's words. That she had even used the word, *'madness'*, was so startling, so deeply intimate that for a moment he felt as if someone had opened his heart for all the world to see. How could she have known that this fear was eating him inside out?

- Other people think—

- What do they think?

- That I've … that I've had a breakdown. That nearly dying in that storm broke me.

- It did break you, Averi. And what a sweet breaking!

Averi looked into Nyx's smile. How white her teeth shone against her skin. How lovely she was, and yet … Averi shook his head and looked away.

- What do Waldo and Hap say? They must talk about it.

- Oh, so you think they're part of my breakdown too?

- I imagine those other people would say so. What do you think?

- I don't wanna talk about them.

- Why not?

- Why not? God, Nyx, wake up and smell the reality. I'm talking to fake people in my head.

- Ever since you were three.

Averi turned, sharply.

- Perhaps if you really look at what they say, you might discover why they have been coming all these years. You said that they don't speak to you as such, but rather speak to each other through you.

- Or about each other; how each behaves.

- Uh huh. Can you—

- I don't wanna talk about them right now.

- Okay.

Averi kicked a pebble into a hard arc.

- I mean it, Nyx.

- Okay.

- Raul says you're a bad influence on me.

Nyx smiled.

- Well, sure, Raul would. But you go with what your intuitive heart tells you, and never mind what anyone thinks. Your mind agrees with Raul, because your mind would rather have you remain locked in fear and ignorance because then it has you controlled. A breakdown might better be termed as a break-*through*, Averi. But, nonetheless, we very often have to be broken in order to see with clear eyes. To be stripped utterly of every concept and idea we have ever had about ourselves and about life is the deepest, most humble surrender that any human can ever undergo. And that means a *stripped person*, who, potentially for some time at least, appears to the world as someone 'altered'. We hold our fear of such surrender even in our language – to be altered is to be what, after all? To be mentally 'unfit'. Be willing to be altered, Averi. In fact, you have no choice, for you *are* altered. And life and you shall never be the same again. You cry because while this feels deeply painful, unsettling and incomprehensible, it also feels deeply true, right and freeing. Some beings find they must retreat; they must walk out of life for a while in order to see Life as it really is. And this only too commonly is seen as some condition to be treated. Think of your father. Did he ever get beyond the label that was given him? No, because his mind found more security in the delusion. But to reach behind this identity and root out all delusion, that is the only task worthy of this life; it is why you were born, Averi. Why we were all born. That is the gift given to human beings: to discover happiness as your own nature.

- But I don't feel happy, Nyx.

- Look at me, Averi. Look at me. I'm not talking about the happiness that comes and goes with the tides. I'm talking about the discovery of your innate Self, your most natural Being whose very flavour is Happiness, Compassion and Love. This I know that you know because I have felt it in you. Do you remember the other day when we were walking down the lane, and when we were sat on the veranda, we discovered that there is something prior to thoughts, prior to all phenomena. And then, to add further spice to our pot, we discovered that this something is not a *thing* at all. Believe me, Nyx smiled, you shall think me a stuck record after not too long, but there is method to this madness; although rather less method and rather more madness, as you shall see. We can confirm together right now if what we discovered is still true. Draw your attention once again to the sense of Existence so intimate to you. It is beyond even intimate, for intimacy suggests, no matter how small, some apparent distance. There is no distance between you and the sense of Existence, because they are one and the same thing. You are not separate from Awareness. You cannot even truthfully say *my* awareness because you *are* Awareness. How can you own what you are? This was your discovery, yes?

- Sure—

- And to be certain that we do not fall into the memory-trap, tell me what is your discovery right now.

- Nyx!

- See this lazy mind. It will do anything to avoid this truth. After all, no mind wants to realise that it is no-*thing*? If you are no-*thing* what on earth could you be?

- I can't sit all day with my eyes shut.

- There is no requirement to sit all day with your eyes shut.

- In my experience there is.

- No, this is your assumption: that any kind of 'spiritual' talk must take place sat, cross-legged, in a quiet, white room, with a gentle mantra playing. All false ideas based on ignorance. Forget spiritual, forget eyes closed, forget everything but the essential, 'I Am'.

- But, I can't feel it otherwise.

- Feel what?

- That feeling of peace. And I agree with you, it felt damn good, but it doesn't last.

- Ah.

Nyx finished the last drops of her coffee and screwed the cup back on top of the flask.

- Are you searching for a nice feeling, or for Absolute Truth?

Averi scoffed and shook his head.

- This is too much for me, man. I'm not clever enough for this.

- Forget clever. Clever only gets you into trouble.

- Seriously, Nyx. My head's gonna explode.

- Whose experience are you talking about?

Averi blew out his cheeks and dropped his head into his hands.

- What?

- You said, 'In my experience you need to sit with your eyes shut.' Identify yourself. *Whose* experience?

- Mine, of course.

- But who is this one to whom the experience belongs?

- God, Nyx, don't speak in riddles. *Me*, Averi!

- And the feeler of peace is who?

- *Me*, Averi.

- Does it help if I ask: the feeler of peace is *what*?

Averi stopped.

- What feels a feeling of peace? Is it your toes?

- Well, okay, my *mind*; my brain.

- Forget 'brain' for the moment. What about this mind? I seem to remember we came to some conclusions the other day about the mind. We saw that the mind thinks. That is the thinking mind's job, after all. To ask it not to think is like asking the wind not to blow. We also saw that thoughts are most often random and non-sequential. We saw their changeability. One minute we feel buoyant, the next we feel irritable; one minute we feel tired, the next we feel adventurous. It is extraordinary when you consider just how many thoughts you can have in one minute alone. Imagine an hour, a day, a lifetime … and the infinite number of changing and inconstant moods, feelings, sensations, emotions and thoughts. You agree?

- Sure.

- So you agree that your mind is always changing its mind?

- Yeah!

- And the other day we discovered that something that is constantly changing cannot in any profound sense be true. So tell me, this mind of yours that is experiencing, if its inconstancy makes it fundamentally untrue, what can you say now about the mind's experience?

- Well, I guess it can't be true either.

Averi stared at Nyx. He was ashamed of his impatience, but somehow he couldn't help himself. Irritation spilled out like rancid wine. He swallowed hard and acidity bit his gut. How patient she was with him, and how little he deserved it. There was that beautiful, smooth skin, the colour of treacle, and the eyes of the dark universe, so deep were their depths. From somewhere he heard her voice.

- What can you say *now* about the mind's experience?

She was smiling at him. It was a smile that cleft his being; an earthquake that turned his eyes outside in, that peeled him inwards like a warm breeze. Averi felt his physical body as it shed its limbs. Like a snake, unsheathed and fresh. That smile bore into him, so deep, that he was not separate from it. Averi saw he *was* smile, boundless, timeless, formless, free. He saw as if he were a witness to his own visual seeing, to his hearing, to his feeling. He saw from the expansiveness of space that he Was. Nothing more: that he Was.

- The mind and its experience are seen from a deeper place.
- Yes.
- They are watched, Nyx.
- And who is the watcher, Averi?
- I am. I am the watcher.
- And *as what* are you?
- I don't know. I don't have words.
- Try. We both know that the wordless can never be truly expressed with words. But they are our closest tool. *As what* are you?
- I am the space that watches.
- And is the space active in any way?
- What do you mean?
- Is the space doing, trying, feeling?
- No. It's not *doing* anything. It's just space.
- Is it watching with interest, or merely impassively?
- It's impassive.
- And what of the one who thinks he is responsible? Remember him?
- He is a thought arising in my mind.
- *He* is a thought?
- Yes.
- So the one that thinks and feels is itself just a thought?
- Yes.
- Can you see, Averi, what you are discovering? You are seeing with your own intuitive eye that the one who thinks – the person, the personality, the 'he', the one who calls himself Averi – is *just a thought*. And thoughts are what?

- They come and they go. They're not real.

- And therefore?

- Averi is not real.

Suddenly Averi burst out, whether with tears or laughter, he was not sure.

- And you, the space that watches, do you feel any sense of responsibility?

But Averi was too overcome to answer.

- Look at me, Averi. Let the emotion come, but don't get sucked in to it. You, the space that watches, do you feel any sense of responsibility?

Averi cried and laughed and wiped his face.

- No.

- No. Space – that innate sense of Existence, that knowing of pure, un-associated Being – is stainless, formless, feeling-less, action-less. It simply Is.

Averi sat quite still, broadened and eyes wide. A stillness that pervaded all throbbed and hummed with the buzz of Existence. It was Silence, absolute and uncontainable Silence.

- Yes, Averi?

- It's as if even this watching is seen in Silence.

- And you, Averi? Where are you?

- I am That. I am the Silence.

Averi saw two tears, one from each eye, fall effortlessly down Nyx's face.

- There now. She smiled, those glints such bright diamonds of love. Beauty, my beloved Averi, as takes your breath away. You see how we have moved out of the land of surmising and into the Heart of pure knowing.

8

⚯

Lydia is sat beside me, leaning her head on her elbow. We have not moved since lunchtime. I am stiff from the hard plastic of the dining chair and she is exhausted after her outburst. I have offered to brush her hair. There was no response. I am learning with Lydia that often the best method is to go ahead and do without waiting for her consent. For example, a few nights ago at supper she refused to eat, or rather this was Anastasia's interpretation. It seemed rather that she had not the will, nor the capacity, to reach for her fork and feed herself. Her arms hung limp, her hands remained in her lap, while her head bowed with depletion. Of course, the more Anastasia berated and the more Reynardo coaxed, the less she was willing to try. Sarah merely tutted and sighed heavily. She is not impressed that the newcomer has taken Jude's place at our table, although she barely acknowledged Jude when he was here. In the end I wondered if I shouldn't try to feed Lydia myself. And, surprisingly, it worked. At first her lips were so unengaged it seemed as if they were new to this game. However, after a few forkfuls, they got the hang of it, and even parted in readiness. She ate then like a child starved. This sparrow needs some serious fattening and so we have organised ourselves a little routine. I take one mouthful from my plate, and then feed her a mouthful from her plate. Despite Anastasia slapping my hand away from time to time, we seem to have hit upon success. We even have our chewings timed into synchrony.

It is coming up to teatime, now. Since Mareka is on duty it is likely we'll have nice biscuits. Anastasia at teatime is a very dull affair; plain digestives or cheap round shortcakes. Everyone knows it for you can feel a general buzz in the direction of the tea table. Four o'clock is approaching, and then it is every man to himself. I have a feeling Lydia and I shall be missing the race. Never mind. If the worst comes to the worst we can always beg Reynardo. He keeps a secret stash of those expensive German biscuits in his bedside table. A slab of dark chocolate on plain rich tea. It makes me smile to think of the little methods of survival in this place. It must feel to these people that if a decent biscuit is the only thing they've got to look forward to, why on earth shouldn't they make a fuss?

What do you have to look forward to, Lydia? Lydia lifts her head as if she has heard my question. The question is, of course, redundant. How addicted we are to looking forward. How obsessively we look to the future as some golden reward; as the happiness that lies around the corner. This subject ended the conversation this morning, between Katherine and I. Hope, and my rebuttal of all its lies. It seemed to hit a nerve. She sat up straight and shot her question at me as if she were armed and ready.

- Why should hope be a lie, she retorted. Surely hope is a source of great comfort, allowing and encouraging progress and movement.

I had not intended to hurt her. But, honestly, she looked as if she were winded. Greg the musician had knocked on the door at that moment and brought our session to a close. So, it was left there hanging in the air, my slap and her bruise, raising and starting to purple.

Lydia is rubbing her eyes with the heels of her hands. When she stops I see how grey the circles are. They are the deep craters of fatigue. And yet, Lydia sleeps. Ten hours last night once the ballad had worn itself out. Fatigue comes because her mind is so fraught. From morning to night it paces with the sleek connivance of a jaguar. Back and forth with senses so finely wrought that her only awareness is the target in sight.

- Stop staring at me.
- I'm sorry.
- What are you doing in here?
- We've been here since lunch, remember?

Lydia looks at me, suspiciously, wanting to see if I am tricking her. My eye darts through the glass wall of the dining room to Mareka in the hallway. She is signalling that Doctor Wood is on his way. Lydia catches my glance and turns to look. Mareka busies herself at the desk, but the inmates are not so careful. One or two look warily down the corridor towards the dining room. Rose, especially, is on high alert. Lydia shakes her head as if she knew all along that I had set her up, and scrapes back her chair in disgust.

- I'm not speaking to Wood.

Doctor Wood is as grey in his demeanour as the walls he so gravely maintains. It is difficult not to sound once again judgemental. But judgement has no place here.

Mine is a concern for these beings who so vehemently shut out life. Lydia is on his case-list and not once in the three weeks of her sat by my side has he ever asked me any questions. He shows no interest in her singing or her paddling feet when the nightmares start; he cares little that she must be spoon-fed and hair-brushed; that this slip of a bird has regressed with all the tenacity of a toddler: one minute, a tantrum; the next, a melting putty of need. No, his concern is for satisfactory response to medication. But how can more be expected when he, like all the rest, has no understanding of the Love that he is?

The jaguar now paces in earnest, and this time in physical form. Her hands are balled and her eyes are face-down, following the direction of her feet. Suddenly, she turns to me and leans on the table.

- Why won't any of you listen to me, she shouts. There is a device in the downstairs lobby, and if someone doesn't go in and switch it off we are all going to be blown to pieces. Jesus, are you deaf?

- I hear you, Lydia. Mareka has phoned down to ask the guy at reception—

- *Mareka!* D'you think I'm gonna trust Mareka?

- She wouldn't lie to you, Lydia.

- She's in with Dmitri, that sly bitch. And you're as dumb as the rest of them if you've let her pull the wool over your eyes.

Lydia says that Dmitri is part of a Russian terrorist network and is working here under false pretext. Last week he was responsible for a Semtex bomb under her bed. As soon as his shift starts now and the spitting begins, the nurses have taken to sedating her. Dmitri takes it all with his kind, long-suffering smile. I wonder how many things he has been accused of in his time.

Whenever Dmitri is around I am careful not to smile back in case I betray her trust. But it seems with the arrival of Wood that I am about to lose it anyway.

- Lydia?

Doctor Wood knocks on the glass. Lydia has barricaded the door with a chair under the handle.

- Will you let me in, please, Lydia?

The stealth of this cat knows no bounds. She bangs at her forehead as she paces.

- In four minutes this entire building will be a fire-ball.

- Lydia, there is no explosive device in the downstairs lobby. I have just spoken to Carl on the desk and he assures me, Lydia—

- If you don't stop saying my name at the beginning and end of every sentence, she screeches, I am going to put my fist through this glass.

And the force of her words does exactly that. At once, Rose in the corridor screams and shoves her fists in her mouth, bringing everyone out into the corridor to watch, while Mareka runs to the supply cupboard.

- You really need to open up the door, now, Lydia.

Perhaps because the deed is done, Doctor Wood doesn't bother to heed Lydia's request. He looks to me and points to the chair.

- If you don't open the door soon, she is going to lose a lot of blood.

- Lili, please, Mareka begs, as she runs back up to the glass. Listen to Doctor Wood.

I am listening, but Lydia is staring at me with those scorched craters, begging me not to betray her. I rush to her side, take off my scarf and wrap it tightly around her wrist. Perhaps she has hit an artery. I don't know anything about such things, but blood is pouring and has soaked through my scarf in no time. Lydia sinks to the ground in shock.

- Lili, she says, you believe me, don't you?

Doctor Wood is shouting now and shaking the door. I have never heard him so animated. He is telling me that the consequences will be severe for me if I hamper Lydia's treatment.

- I believe you, of course I do.

- The bomb, Lili, is in the bottom drawer in the left-hand filing cabinet. We're all gonna die.

- No, Lydia, we're not all going to die. I'm going to go and find it.

- You'll have to defuse it.

- I can do that.

- Do you know how?

- I've never done it before, but if you talk me through it I can. Doctor Wood, are you listening?

- Open up at once!

Lydia is going limp in my arms.

- There are only three minutes left, she says. You'll have to be quick.

- Doctor Wood, Lydia says there is an explosive device downstairs in the lobby in the left-hand filing cabinet. She says there are only three minutes left before it goes off, so you're going to have to listen to me. I need you to let me out so that I can try to defuse it. I can phone up to the nurses' desk from Carl's phone and Lydia can talk me through it.

I can see Doctor Wood frozen on the end of incredulity. Mareka is turning and exhorting him to say yes. I can see how worried she looks at the sight of Lydia's blood. The doctor looks utterly bewildered. Surely, this is not beyond the realm of his expertise.

- We're running out of time, Doctor. Do you really want us all to die?

He looks to me, to Mareka, to Lydia and then back to me.

- Very well, very well.

Lydia looks up at me with such gratitude as she nods, that instinctively I bend forward and kiss her.

- We'll be fine, I say. We're going to make it.

And I run to the door, throw back the chair as Mareka rushes in, and push through the crowd to the exit. It takes Doctor Wood another moment to see that I am serious. He looks so baffled I want to kiss him too.

- It's okay, I say. We'll be fine. Make sure Lydia is by the phone.

He lets me out and I race to the stairs, not bothering for the lift, and hurtle three flights as if life and limb were against that timer.

- Carl! I shout, give me the phone!

Poor Carl, the security guy, is so startled from his newspaper that he barely has a moment to react. I press the key for Saffron Ward.

- When I give you the sign, Carl, I want you to open up the left-hand filing cabinet.

- What?

- Just do it! Lydia! It's me, it's Lili. Okay.

I nod to Carl, who open-mouthed, and wide-eyed, does as he is told. No doubt this is all in a day's work with mental patients. Luckily, the heavy drawer scrapes on its rollers and Lydia can hear it.

- Lydia, I'm here. Now quickly, what do I do?

Her voice is faint and I can hear the blood running out of her.

- Okay, you should be able to see three wires.

- Three wires?

And I nod to Carl, who bizarrely looks to the drawer of files and nods in agreement.

- The middle one should be orange. You need to cut that one.

- The orange? You sure, now? Carl, have you got any pliers?

- Yeah, I'm sure, whispers Lydia.

- Okay, wait, Carl is just finding the— Okay, he's got them. I've got them!

- Fifteen seconds, Lili. Fifteen seconds.

- My hands are shaking, Lydia. My hands are shaking.

- You can do it, Lili. You can do it!

The clock on the wall hits four and even though it doesn't chime, with marvellous exactitude a distant church bell announces teatime. My hands really are shaking on the end of the phone.

- I've got it, I'm *cutting*! It's done, Lydia, it's done. We're safe, now.

And I mime to Carl to slide back the drawer, which he does with just enough noise to reassure her.

9

A butterfly has been here since this morning. It flew into my room and woke me in time for breakfast. He is beautiful – a peacock – with his burnt orange colour and blue-specked orbs, like the four eyes of the universe on his back. He startled me at first with impatience, it seemed, as he flicked his wings about my face. But I don't think even Dmitri believed me – a butterfly in November, in a place without windows – for the peacock was not to be seen all day. Now he is back. Flat upon the wall above Lydia's lamp, the night light tickling his antennae. She hasn't seen him yet. She is too afraid of her nightmare. This latest is the most frequent. And it comes with the same vision.

- Can you describe it, I ask.
- Not really, she says. Only a lack of solidity.
- What do you mean by that?
- I don't know.
- Why is it frightening?
- *Because*, she urges, there is no solidity.

I wait for her to settle. We mustn't wake the ward.

- Can you describe what you see? – Lydia?

- I don't know.

- You say the feeling comes with a vision.

She looks up at me and meets my eye as if she were seeing me very clearly for the first time.

- You know on science programmes when they show images of the electrical activity of the brain?

- Yes?

- It's like that. No solidity. Just electrical impulses shooting out across a network of transmitters.

I am sat opposite Lydia on her bed, crouched in the same position. I am struck in that moment how adult she is; how the frightened child has disappeared. But almost the instant I see it, she starts to shake and her eyes are lost.

- Can you tell me what you are feeling right now?

- Anxiety.

- Okay.

I take her hand and she holds mine tight.

- Can you tell me what is aware of your anxiety?

- I am.

- What do you mean by you?

- My innocence. The love that I am.

My heart stops to hear it.

- But, they're coming.

- Who are coming?

- The ones who want to kill me.

- Yes.

- They know the code to get in here.

- So, we'll be waiting for them, together, okay?

Her eyes strain to see if I am telling the truth. My own heart is pumping so loudly I can barely breathe. Did you ever hear such perfection? Spoken so unselfconsciously, as if she had not even heard her own words. *My Innocence. The Love that I Am.*

   - Lydia?

I stopped myself a few moments ago. Words were so close on the end of my tongue they were almost dancing. She is lying down on her side now and I am lying behind her, stroking her hair. I wish the world could see what I have just seen. How clear it is that this mind will go to any lengths to avoid the Self, even in the immediate seconds after Truth is expressed. Especially, I mean, after Truth has spoken. She barely took a breath before the story kicked in. What other proof do we need that this is the human journey?

   - Lydia?

It feels like the movement of colliding worlds about to express itself. Some rein is holding me in the pit of my knowing, but it is no good. *This* world is about to overspill itself. Even if she is asleep, it matters little; for the words are pumped and eager.

   - Do you know what I see in you? I see the Love that you are; I see your Innocence, beyond your physical you. You say that your nightmare reveals a lack of solidity. But Lydia, do you know what you are discovering? There is nothing to be afraid of, but I understand your fear. That there might not be any substance to the world seems utterly terrifying to your mind. And your mind will do anything to avoid this truth. For this is what you have seen. Your own intuition, appearing to you in your dreaming state, has revealed that this whole material existence has no solidity. What wisdom in that seeing, Lydia, if only you knew it. Of course, you *do* know it; this 'You' which you yourself described as 'the love that you are', as 'your own innocence', this 'You' knows all. Keep your attention here. That which is aware of your anxiety is aware of all your thoughts and feelings and experiences. Look and see if the Innocence is anxious. Look and see if the Innocence is frightened. Trust me, dearest Lydia; I speak only as Love to Love. Who is the real killer you are afraid of? This question will light a fire in you; it will burn all delusion, all falsity to the ground. Who is this killer? This is a story your mind has constructed to keep you from knowing your Self. And yet the genius of your creation is that recognition of Self will, indeed, kill. It shall kill all ideas of the mind. It will destroy you and all you think yourself to be. Be willing to be destroyed, Lydia, so that you may taste the Freedom that you are, the Love that you are, the Innocence that you are.

This fire is so stoked I might just combust. How much I want this bird to sing.

I sit up on my elbow and listen to her breathing. I notice for the first time the ticking of her alarm clock. It seems to move in sync with my pulse. I do a double-take to see my butterfly friend come to rest on the stroke of three, those four eyes quivering like a question. Suddenly Lydia is moving her arm and pulling her hair from her face. The arm comes to rest and I wait some more. But neither of us speaks another word.

10

It is not yet time for weekly rounds, but Katherine is early. She is standing at the foot of my bed, ticking through the usual list of questions, and nodding without looking up to my list of side-effects: tremors, pain in my joints, constipation, dizziness, daily headaches, irregular heartbeat, alternate restlessness and sleepiness, and this morning I vomited again. The doctors say that all these are standard reactions to the medication, along with agitation, anxiety and hallucination; rather peculiar effects when one considers the idea is to *stop* so-called hallucination and anxiety. Oh well, who am I to challenge medical expertise? Doctor Kolinsky will prescribe a laxative for the constipation, painkillers for the headaches and will keep an eye on the vomiting. She is now considering changing my anti-psychotics despite my persistent request to stop them. Patient preference plays no part in this game. If I were a cancer patient and instructed my oncologist that I no longer wished to continue treatment I do believe that would be my right. But in this grey area of medical science the mental patient seems to have been denuded of all rights. The over-reaching argument is to make sure that patients are not a violent risk to themselves or to anyone else. I think I can safely say that we have all at some point unconsciously committed emotional violence towards those who love us and even towards those who don't, not to mention against ourselves. The great learning is to bring this behaviour into the light of enquiry and to investigate its source. As for physical violence, goodness, I hope that the only violence I have ever committed to persons known and unknown was to have caused them the unnecessary pain of worry for my welfare. That in itself is burden enough, and for that I am, or at least was, truly sorry. I say 'was', because now I see that the apparent suffering of those who witnessed an apparent breakdown was a part of their learning. It is sheer arrogance to try to alter their path. All I can do is reside in the Heart. No action that emerges from Truth can ever truly damage. However, I realise I have stepped away from what is happening right now and have fallen into what Katherine terms 'distant reverie', in which I appear to sink so far inside myself that a line and hook would be hard pushed to reach me.

- What are you reading?

Katherine's voice brings me back to my room. I look down at the dusky pink cover of the romance novel that Rose has lent me. It has upon it an impoverished young girl, painted against the harsh Northern background of a Victorian mill-town. In fact, it is more accurate to say that Rose *instructed* me to read it. She is addicted to the romance novel and since I am the only one who listens to her as she relates each and every detail of the characters and their exploits, she now wishes that I read so that I can see what she sees. There is the young innocent called Jemima who is being courted by a mill-worker, Stan. Tough and honest, with a heart as broad as his weaving arm-span, our resilient Stan must save his love from the wicked intentions of Hugo, the mill-owner's handsome son. I mock, but in fact although the characters are pretty silly, somehow I find myself immersed in a very convincing world of Lancashire mill-workers circa 1840. In a strange way I find myself moved by it. Actually, it isn't strange: not when you consider all former ideas have been shaken from their moorings and nothing is as it was.

- It's one of Rose's, I say, and turn the cover to show Katherine.

Katherine nods, but I see now that she is not really interested in what I am reading. She has stepped towards the desk and the cabinet above and is looking, as if for clues. She has remarked before that this room is conspicuously bare; no pictures, posters, or photographs, no personal knick-knacks to make me feel at home. I came here with nothing and continue so. Given my love of words, she once said, she was particularly surprised by the lack of books. The only object of sentiment is a glazed ceramic bowl made for me by Reynardo in art class. Katherine turns it slightly so that the bright red letters of Lili face front. Now *she* turns, puts my file and her pen on my desk and indicates the chair.

- May I?

- Of course.

I sit up straight in bed and wrap the blanket around me. Despite the thermometer on permanent bake in this place, today I feel chilled. Something is in the air.

I watch my doctor as she crosses her legs, slim and well-toned in a grey silk pencil skirt. She is restless I see;

those wings are palpitating; those cornflowers fluttering, skittish on a light breeze.

- There is love in this room. You're quite safe.
- Why should I not feel safe, she retorts.

No words come out, so we sit in silence.

There is some sort of a kerfuffle in the hallway. Katherine and I look to one another as we listen to Greg whooping and exclaiming with joy about something. Suddenly my door bursts open and there stands Greg looking taller and brighter than a thousand Gregs, his blond tufty hair standing up on end and his long gangly arms cradling a classical guitar.

- He bought one, Lili! Look! He bought me one!

He means his brother who has been requested by the staff not to bring in a guitar. Perhaps the brother finally caved after three months.

- That's wonderful, Greg. Now you can show us what you can do.
- Look at the inlay! Oh, Lili, it's a beauty.
- It's so delicate. He's got good taste, your brother.
- That he has. Oh man!
- I'm really happy for you, Greg.

His chin is wobbling.

- You'd better keep it out of Anastasia's way.

Greg laughs to stop himself from crying and shakes his head as he carries it like a dream out of the room.

- I wonder how long this one will last.

There is no spite in her words. Nonetheless, Katherine looks as if she is checking herself. What she is referring to is the history of guitar-smashing. The last one went straight through the office window. It and much glass collided with Anastasia and her lunch; and hot coffee scalded her thigh. I shall suggest to Greg later that he hide it under his bed and only play it when Dmitri and Mareka are on duty.

Katherine is looking at me, as if waiting for me to speak. There is something on her mind, I see that. I have a feeling it's to do with our last session. She has that same startled look about her. I feel *my* mind starting to anticipate. So I settle in the Heart and stay silent.

- Before you came, Lili, patients very rarely interacted. Well, to be frank, they still don't, but they interact with you. Even when you were silent and refused to speak they were … quieter somehow in your presence. I'd like to know why.

This question cost her a great deal, I can see by the shortening of her breath. I wonder how long she has been trailing it behind her. She certainly looks exhausted by it. Once again I am struck by how fragile she looks, this red-haired angel, looking, yet not looking, as she straightens the rope-like tassels of her scarf on her lap. If only, sweet Katherine, you knew of your own divine harmony. She lifts her head, now, and addresses me directly.

- I once asked Reynardo why he seeks your company. He told me it was because you never judge him. I see now that perhaps that is what the others too feel. Rose and her books; Greg and his music; and Lydia.

- And you?

- What of me?

- What do you feel in my presence?

- I am your doctor, Lili.

- And doctors don't feel?

What a struggle there is going on. My mind wants to jump in and articulate it for her; yet my heart knows to wait. It tells me to change the subject.

- I wanted to thank you again for the walk. You should have seen Reynardo's face. He was so excited.

- And you, Lili? What was your experience? You have told me of Reynardo's, but not of your own.

- We just caught the last of the colours. It was so lovely. I had not imagined I would miss it so much.

- How could you not miss being outside?

This question comes out fast and unrestrained, as if for half a second Katherine had revealed herself. It suddenly occurs to me that perhaps this place, this asylum, is secretly this doctor's worst fear: to be locked in, disbelieved, without escape.

- What I am, I reply, is neither inside nor outside. I am neither free nor un-free. In the most profound sense, wherever you put me, I remain untouched.

I see her intake, as if she thought we were, for one moment, really conversing, only to lose me to riddles. I wish I did not confuse her so. But there is no choice: whatever that 'something' *is* in the air, it is pushing, urgently.

- That said, the body and mind crave beauty. This is natural. Without it we as people are barren. Does it never alarm you that a place such as this strangles all attempts at beauty? Does it never occur to you that an eight by six grey box should sever the artery of life in these beings? Lydia and Rose and Reynardo, they are not ready to be put 'anywhere'. They must be put where there is love. They seek me out because I see their Perfection, the Love that they are.

- You see mental illness as perfection?

- That's not what I'm saying.

- So, what on earth are you seeing as perfection?

- I see *you* as Perfection, but not merely the personal you. I see you both as the personal you and the Impersonal You.

- Do you see yourself as mentally ill?

- Of course not. Do you? Because I know you're beginning to question that.

Katherine shoots a look so sharp it hurts.

- Lili, I came in early to see you today because I don't feel that I should continue as your psychiatrist. Under the circumstances—

- What circumstances?

- Well, I think we both see that not much progress is being made here. No one is to blame. Sometimes doctors and patients consider there to be less harm done by admitting defeat and going elsewhere.

- Do you feel I am *harming* you? Because I don't feel you are harming me.

She is holding herself so tight it is unbearable to watch.

- You said yourself that you don't believe in hope.

- I didn't say that.

- Perhaps that is my fault. You need a doctor who at least instils hope in you; otherwise you will never leave this place.

- First of all, I've told you that I don't believe in anything; and second, what I said about hope is that it is the great lie to humanity.

- As long as you speak in these grandiose terms we get nowhere. What on earth does that mean, 'the great lie to humanity'? It may sound intelligent, but all it does is keep you at a distance, keep you from ever speaking truthfully.

- Katherine, the Truth of which I speak is beyond even the concept of truth.

Katherine shakes her head, grabs my file and her pen, and stands to go.

- But I see now why you label me with these delusions of grandeur. I understand how I must sound. My words are a foreign language to you. But just because something is foreign doesn't make it wrong or crazy or delusional. I can tell you most earnestly that these words are anything but grand. What they point to is the most humble and simplest truth.

- I shall hand your case file over to Doctor Wood.

- I don't want to speak with Doctor Wood.

- I have persuaded him to return your walking privileges, despite the Lydia debacle.

- May I speak to you now about hope? Do you want to understand why I denounce this idea called hope? I see you, Katherine.

In front of the door now, hand on handle, Katherine looks back, defiantly.

- Yes, I do. And may I tell you what I see? Perhaps, I should not have spoken so freely with you over these months, but somehow when words must be said they come without interference. I know that if you walk out that door you may never face *that* which you are here to face.

- That which I—

- Be furious; it's good that you are. At last a window has opened and enquiry has begun. You, like the others you described, feel drawn to my Presence. I know that must sound the most egotistical of statements, but the simple truth is that it is beyond ego. What I really mean to say – though you shall accuse me of talking in riddles – is that you are drawn to the Presence I am; to the Presence that emanates out of this being. You don't understand this pull; it terrifies and comforts you at the same time. You look to your manuals and your training and it appears I tick all the boxes. How easy it should be to make your conclusions. But you cannot. You cannot arrive at one single conclusion because they all now appear to you as false. Everything you once understood is coming apart at the seams. Your only recourse is to run, lest you be swamped with the terror of not knowing anything any more.

- And all this because of you, she says derisively.

- No, because of *you*. Your own Self is calling out to Self. What a divine calling! You are merely witnessing your Self in me. Just like Bill and Rose and Greg, you are drawn to the hum of Existence itself. And your mind, like all minds in the history of the human species, is a bolting horse.

There are tears gathering in those ragged cornflowers, but Katherine shall fight them. She lifts the clipboard, clicks the end of her pen and writes at the bottom of the page.

- I've already requested an increase of dose—

- Shall I tell you now about hope? Hope is a lie because it insists upon a fictitious future. Hope is the stuff of the mind and bolsters the mind and reassures the mind and keeps human beings forever believing in the mind. How extraordinary that you, a scientist of the mind, do not even know what *Mind* is. Hope keeps you away from now, and always striving for something else. It keeps you in anticipation, in expectation; it keeps you trapped in desire and wanting, a never-ending painful quagmire of suffering and delusion. Hope is the real delusion, and my God, are human beings full of it. Cast off hope, be utterly hope-less, and then you might actually live. What are you without it? Ask that question, Katherine, and then you shall *know beyond knowing* who you are. I say these words not to be clever, not to outsmart you or trick you. Forget clever; clever only gets you into trouble. What I am pointing to is beyond intellectual knowledge. Be willing to be perfectly stupid, Katherine. Yes! As ridiculous as that sounds! For one moment be willing to let go of the reins. Because it seems to me you have come to the choice-less choice: to hang up those spurs of the intellect and finally to remain still. I understand your fear; trust me, I do. I understand why you look at me now, horrified, as if I had cut off your air supply. But let me cut it off, Katherine, I beg of you, so that you may learn to breathe your own Truth.

11

The one and perhaps only redeeming quirk of my room is that it catches the late afternoon sun. Today is a particular joy. That golden, tarnished look, which steeps the landscape in warm sepia, is sliding like a seraph across my bedspread. The edge of its sixth wing is brushing the legs and lap of Katherine Kolinsky. She is sat now with a saucer on her knee, drinking tea like a bird on a bath.

Dearest Reynardo brought the tea. His keen antennae must have sought us out. It did make me smile to see his spiky bristle of grey appearing at the glass in my bedroom door. A twitch of my head was enough to warn him. Then, with just a two-handed mime of a teacup and saucer, and one stretched look across to Katherine, Reynardo was on the case. It was so sweet how he bent in silence as he entered the room. He gave the tea to me, knowing it was for Katherine. It breaks my heart to see how he picks up on the detail.

We are alone again now but for the seraph. I don't think Katherine has noticed him. But I must be patient. She has taken in so much already. It is enough that she let go of the handle; that her eyes met mine, full and frightened; that she sat on the chair in silence. We are in such new territory that neither of us has any idea of footing. I see that the tea has calmed her. Her chest is falling normally now, though clearly she is exhausted. It is a strange but subtle distinction to see the difference of energy between one depleted and one spent. There is space in a person spent. Depression gone; no impetus yet. A fresh hinterland of emptiness.

My body is still chilled; so chilled in fact that it has gone into a spasm of inner shivering. My position on the bed keeps me out of the sun. But, I don't mind. Today this warmth is for Katherine. And besides I have a feeling not even a six-winged seraph could heat this me. Cold has set in for a reason. As I wrap the blanket around me, I see so clearly this human frailty: how, Katherine, you shroud yourself in your suffering, as if pain could be your shield. Hand it over, sweet Katherine. If only you could see the perfection of this timing; how the light is stretching itself over your head, like a sleek ribbon of enquiry. You are too weighted to know, your head still bowed, your eyes fixed, in full possession of identity. Hand it over, I pray, and let the tide take you where it wills.

12

〰

All he knew was that he shook. And the oddest sensation of falling through a worm-hole. A perfectly cylindrical tunnel that curved and distorted its own direction through space. All around was blackness, save for some kind of iridescence that marked the edges of the tunnel. There was a voice, alternately distant and close; what sounded like the incessant opening and shutting of doors; and an unbearable heaviness of something pressing down upon him. The voice now drew that heaviness back. What a relief to feel his limbs free and exposed. Until the cold shook them out of existence.

But what a ride – oh boy – on the arrow of time! It was a rabbit hole with its own momentum, for all at once it shot upwards, steered a sharp course left, or undulated with the perfect ripple of wind-spun desert. And what did he see? So fast they came, such images of peoples and cities, a marching army, a wild stallion and a great noose flung about its neck; a longhouse in a wide prairie expanse, a fire outside and a young boy sitting and crying over a dead fawn in his lap; an old woman at a cottage hearth, her table full of herbs, a sharp smell of marjoram, rosemary and thyme; an even sharper tang of goats, a herd of them, their fenced enclosure in verdant countryside; a young woman crossing to the gate to meet an approaching rider on horseback; and back to the innards of this arrow through time.

A heat now came, such a burning. He knew that his body flailed to be free of it, but it raged all the same. His skin was raw and tight to the bone. Flames were running the course of his veins, he heard himself curse them. Some secret part of him told him he was licked, to let the fire devour him; that there was nothing to be done but to let this one burn to the ground. But the fighter resisted. He would not give in to this enemy. He thrashed and grappled and refused to bow down. But it was no use. No battle cry could have sundered this fire.

And so he surrendered, more out of exhaustion than will. He felt his body, as it shook, give in. In fact, it was a sweet giving. He had not imagined it would be so sweet. His body was so light it brushed the air like sun-dust. When he tried he could not even touch it. He was but the air that danced, until the closer he looked the less he saw. He was the space that neither danced nor stood still. Oh, what a discovery! He saw this body as somehow distinct from himself, and yet at the same time not distinct. Oh, what a mystery! All appeared before him, before this space-like Self, effortless and without pull. He was but *sight*, a disembodied witness to the whole of manifestation. The divine note had struck its chord and he was that blissful chime. Its vibration did not move through him, it *was* him. Out of this one pure note, he knew, was born this entire visible universe.

Birth and dissolution were born out of *him*. Movement moved, sound sounded, senses sensed, listening listened, feelings felt, emotions emoted, thoughts thought, all of this he saw without preference, without inclination, without effort. He that witnessed the movement was not the movement, and yet was not separate from it either. Oh, what a hum! The changeable changed in front of him, but he himself was unchanging; the world before him was bright and vivid with difference and variety, but he himself was undifferentiated; forms were born into time and space, but he himself was timeless, formless; billions of worlds thought and breathed, but he himself was prior to the world; he's and she's and personal identities went about their business, but he, the *Self,* was neither he, nor she, nor a personal identity. He, him-*Self,* was the hum of Existence in which an identity of a *him* was born. How else was the One to taste itself if not through the multiplicity of the many? And, oh boy, what a taste! What a nectar it was! Not the ephemeral happiness of worldly life that comes and goes like ships on a breeze, but the constant, unmoving, boundless Freedom, of Peace, of Compassion, of Love.

PART THREE

1

‍

W hat a cheeky surprise! Reynardo has a new hat, given to him by his mother, Florence. He looks like our Christmas tree in his olive green duffle and his hat the colour of maraschino cherries. There's no danger of him being missed on a dark winter's night, that's for sure. His face split into stars when Florence arrived. There she stood in a tweed overcoat with the collars turned up, a chenille scarf all the colours of the rainbow, her fingers heavy with crystals, raising her arms with joy at the sight of our limp and sorry tree. No one but Rose has paid the Christmas decorations any attention so far. She is probably still there, dear Rose, in her pink dressing gown, re-arranging the colours into groups.

The present is two weeks early because Florence shall be away in Sheffield in panto over the Christmas holidays. In fact, the run lasts until the end of February. How marvellous to see this eighty-seven-year-old's zest for life. Reynardo beamed as she told him all about the cast, those she liked, those she whispered should not be allowed within a fifty-mile radius of a stage, and those she had worked with in 1957. The set was wonderful, but the lighting a travesty, she said, as she laid down her winning hand of gin rummy on the tea table. All three of us – myself, Reynardo and Lydia - put up our hands: this was the third time in a row that Florence had won. Lydia, disgruntled and obviously not aware of the game within the game, got up and stomped away. Florence rubbed her hands with glee, while Reynardo scraped the cards all together and shuffled for a new draw. It was a gentle routine, loving and understated, despite the actress and her role. She even played along happily with the Lili game without batting an eyelid.

What was so beautiful to observe was that, despite their devotion, there was nonetheless a detachment within this mother towards her son. It did not make her less loving; on the contrary, her love was free and openly expressed. The distance, paradoxically, allowed it to flow. Florence loved her boy precisely as he was, without wishing to change him. How amazing to see such trust in life. She caught my eye as she dealt the next round, and that warm glint said it all.

- I don't understand.

- No, I know. It's a mystery, isn't it? How a mother can mother without being 'mother'.

I look at Katherine across the interview table. She is playing with that ring on her index finger.

- How a wife can be a wife without being 'wife'.

She stares straight at me now.

- How a daughter can be a daughter without being 'daughter'. Detachment shall not make you any less of a mother, any less of a wife, or daughter. In fact, what is discovered is that the roles may be played quite beautifully, effortlessly, freely, without the mess of identification. First find out who you are prior to being a wife or a doctor, even prior to being a woman. Then from this new perspective you may begin to uncover the layers of each of those roles and really understand the level of identification for each. These are your tools for stripping yourself back to your Self.

- What are?

- The roles you play, your traits, your relationships, your life as you know it.

Katherine is biting the inside of her upper lip. I am going too fast. It is my fault for jumping in and talking about Florence. Today is Friday. On Monday morning, Dmitri came into my room with the message that Doctor Kolinsky had booked the interview room for the two of us every day this week, ten until twelve. Dmitri had smiled at my surprise, and had then given me the strangest – and sweetest – nod of recognition. Each morning he opened up and then each day at twelve he knocked on the door to let me know that the room was needed. We both knew I was not obliged to wait for her, but it seemed as well to sit here as any place. I knew that Katherine would not be rushed even in her own arrangements. So, when I arrived this morning and found her waiting for me, there was no need of explanation. She had taken the chair facing the window, her back to the door. It seemed strange at first since this is always my chair, as if she were deliberately putting me in the doctor's spot. But now that I am sitting in this new position, facing the window in the door, I can see why. It is very exposed. Figures are constantly passing; some even look in as they pass. Greg has already turned back for a second look, stunned to see me and not Katherine in the chair. Clearly, word has got out.

Rose, Sarah and Reynardo have each taken their turn, Reynardo in particular making it known how impressed he was. He lifted a great thumbs-up and grinned like I had scored a goal. There is, though, no goal to be scored. On the contrary, seeing Katherine, small and vulnerable, across the table, stripped of files and pens and her doctor's pose, even stripped of her glasses, is to experience a moment of privilege. Whatever brought her here today I must be delicate in my unpeeling, so as not to sabotage this opportunity. She looks tired, and strange as it may sound, I am glad. There is a sort of imposed willingness to her exhaustion that I suspect shall give us room.

Nevertheless, it is confirmed once again what a subtle manipulator is this mind. I see how my mind jumped in to fill the silence with my story about Florence. In those quiet minutes after Katherine's arrival an anxiety arose that I should help bridge this gap between us. It was so fast that I barely registered it. But in that instant, my mind jumped in to be the doer; it did not trust that words will come when they come. Even this one who has such good intentions is a fake and not to be trusted. How evident it is that goodness manifests spontaneously. What need is there of a pusher? Katherine Kolinsky has already made the most auspicious of steps. Consciousness has everything in hand. I shall merely be an arm to lean on.

- And so, she asks now, what of Reynardo? His mother's detachment doesn't seem to have left him any less attached to her. How does it help him?

I look to those cornflowers and see their confusion. I am reminded of Florence and her patience. Even Lydia's tantrum had revealed it. After Lydia had scraped her chair back and stormed away from the card table she had knocked into Greg and nudged the neck of his guitar. He had shouted at her to be careful, rocking his prize in his arms like an infant. Lydia had yelled, but you don't even play it, so what does it matter if it gets knocked? It is true that Greg doesn't play his guitar. He carries it about with him at all times; he has been seen shaping chords and lovingly running notes along the board. But, he says, he daren't play as long as there is a chance that the rage will come. He cannot risk destroying this one. This he had explained to Florence, who had listened as she laid out the cards. It is a shame, she'd said, for I hear you are a real virtuoso; but I understand there is a timing to these things that cannot be rushed. Why don't you join us for a game? But Greg had been forming sequences by this point and had not seemed to hear her.

- It helps Reynardo immeasurably, I say.

Katherine raises an eyebrow.

- And this you know?

- Like I said, it's immeasurable. It shall be helping in ways that are not ours to see.

Katherine exhales, carefully.

- Reynardo has his own path. His attachment is his own, to discard or not discard. And chances are in this lifetime he may not.

- In this lifetime?

Her tone makes me wobble; or rather, *I* make me wobble, and I know to bring my mind to my Heart.

- Lifetimes are not our concern now.

- What is our concern?

For some reason, an answer doesn't come. But it sits there, nonetheless, pulsating on a wire. Once more I can feel the urgency, so urgent I can taste it. That red lock has slipped free again. Katherine pushes it behind her ear and presses her lips together.

- This word you use ... *identification*.

Her consonants are crisp and wary. She waits, as if for my parry.

Words are coming. I feel them like a train. This time there shall be no manipulation.

2

~**W**ell, hi there.
      The light was so bright that Averi was momentarily blinded.

- Geez, that's right in your eye. Let me pull that.

Nyx was leaning over the divan and pulling at a cord. Slats came down and Averi blinked. It took him a few moments to focus. What came sharpest out of all his senses was smell. A wonderful buttery smoke with the deep earthy tang of mushrooms. Averi had never in his life felt so hungry, or hankered more for that earthy taste. Nyx was busy at a central counter cracking eggs into a bowl. Plates were already laid at the table. There were fat slices of wholemeal toast, butter in a dish and a pot of damson jam. Averi wondered if he were imagining it. He hadn't had damsons since he was a boy. He lifted himself off his elbow so that he was upright. His head was light and his limbs were stiff, but the pain in his joints had gone now. Slowly, he spun himself around so that his feet touched the floor. There in a pile was a stack of his sweaters, his twill shirts and corduroys. And on the top, one next to the other, were two thick red-and-green stripy socks. Averi smiled at the break in his throat and looked up to see Nyx watching him.

- Patch brought them. Well, you sweated yourself out of your other clothes.

Aware now that he was naked to the waist, Averi threw on a sweater and some corduroys, pulled the blanket around his shoulders and crossed to the table. The smell that came next was so good that Averi thought he must have died and gone to heaven. Nyx had turned off the gas on the stove and was pouring black coffee from a metal pot into two mugs.

- There's cream and sugar if you want it.

But Averi liked it just as it was. He steeped his nose in the musky steam and drank; burning, bitter and delicious.

- How many days was I—

- Four, Nyx cut him off. Long enough to need some feeding.

And she put down a plate in front of him – mushrooms fried in butter, grilled tomatoes, creamy omelette with onions and parsley, and little potatoes baked in their skins. Averi cut a slab of butter and smeared it over the potatoes. Nothing was better than this. Neither waited on ceremony, both ate in silence; though Averi did have the feeling that he was watched. Once his plate was clear and he had finished his second slice of toast and jam, he looked up to see that Nyx was only halfway through. Then he felt ashamed that perhaps he had rushed and eaten without care. But Nyx didn't seem to mind. She smiled over her coffee mug at his plate wiped clean of juice.

- Is life any less enjoyable now that you have discovered you are Nothing?

She was laughing inwardly at her joke, that slightly anarchic glint shining like a challenge.

- No, smiled Averi. And he meant it.

3

~**S**ome say that to know Truth is to know madness. You have claimed many times that in the first few months of my being here I refused to speak. This is not true. I didn't refuse; it was simply that there was no inclination to speak. It was not a choice as such, merely that words were not available, at least not of the audible kind. Now they come. However extraordinary they may sound, the best thing you can do is trust that they are pure, and see where their wisdom takes us. That way you shall not be so frightened when I say that to know Truth is to know madness. To be fair, this makes no sense unless we first of all define madness. It is of little use to anyone to bandy about such a term without understanding its meaning. Let us consider three definitions that are easily confused. The first is this: the human being is convinced that he is his mind, or I should say, his *conditioned* mind. He is convinced that his thoughts, feelings, memories, emotions are a summation of his entire self. He is convinced that he is a body and mind and nothing more. He is addicted to thinking and to believing his thoughts. This, we shall perhaps discover together, is pure delusion. Thoughts are not real in any profound and lasting sense. Therefore the one who believes in such unreality might be considered mad, no? Do not trouble yourself with trying to remember or understand; all of this we shall return to.

The second definition is as follows: pure – one might even dare to call it *divine* madness – is to be disembodied, disembowelled and disinherited of everything you know and think that you know about yourself and about life. It is a bitter irony that the *unravelling* of this delusion called the *mind* is considered by those truly deluded to be a delusion! More than that, it is considered an illness in need of a cure. What a great master of ceremonies is this Consciousness that it must invent such playful ways to get our attention. But this is the trick, Katherine. Our intuition must find a chink in all the obstruction if we are to allow our attention to be caught. For our attention is forever drawn to this and that and whatever appeals to the momentary satisfaction. To pierce that layer is therefore a moment of Grace in itself. This is your opportunity to see through the great play of Life. It seems Life is calling you to Life. In that sense what choice do you have? But, as I have said, awakening to the nature of who you are is a painstaking disenfranchisement; not a cell shall remain intact as it was; not a single thing shall be left to you. It may be perceived as a messy and bloody affair, Katherine, but even more so if you struggle. Far better, I say, to let the axe fall. Unfortunately, most beings tend to struggle. Although, whether it is unfortunate or not is hardly the point. Each of us, so it appears, has a path to tread on the road to Truth. But, nevertheless, the struggle, in whichever way it manifests, leads us to our third definition of madness.

The turning of your back on Love, on Truth, on recognition of your true nature is man's route to insanity. We see it all around us, and not just in a psychiatric ward. Why do you think there is such mayhem out there? Beings are beside themselves, but they don't have any idea what they are beside themselves about. They feel something is wrong, and they look to the world and blame the world. My goodness, even our language expresses our delusion – to be 'beside oneself', that is not to be *in* oneself – is the language of craziness, of breakdown, of disorder. And yet, conversely, the very distance of being a witness to one's own mind is peace itself. What a mix-up! I know the struggle in you, Katherine; you look at me and wonder what brought me to this brink? How could you, a doctor of psychiatry, be drawn to this presence? For that is what it is, my *Presence*, not my personality. My personality holds nothing for you. The fact is, you can't explain what makes you sit, or what allows you even to listen to these words when such a strong voice in you warns they are the words of the psychotic, the deluded, the sick. Yet something formless, timeless, imageless, description-less calls you. I do not wish to trick you, or goad you, or make you feel any less than. I merely urge you to trust that I speak only as Love. For what I see in you is Perfection.

We have a stumbling block, though. No matter how strongly you feel drawn to me there is a potent voice that wants you first of all to know if you can trust me as a human being, let alone as a psychiatric patient. After all, who am I to try to tell you who you are? And you'd be right for thinking so. My sole advice to you is never to believe anything I say; don't ever take my word for it. This is *your* discovery to be made. This must be your own direct experience. To bring the mind to the Heart is to fall in love with your Self. My *words* can never persuade anyone. To be drawn to my Presence is merely to be drawn to your Self. But since, to begin with at least, it shall appear that my words are guiding you, it is only fair that you have an idea of what brought me here; of my so-called path.

I did not ask to wake up, Katherine. Does a sleeper know to wake? Unconsciously, some spring kicks into action and tells the sleeper it is time. In fact, what I am is neither awake nor un-awake, but for ease of parlance I shall say that, yes, I awoke. It was not a blinding light, there was no archangel Gabriel, but there was – how can I say it – a precise moment of absolute dropping in which only one certainty remained: that all beings were somehow merged in essence and that I was not separate from them. The deeper realisation that there is, in truth, no 'I' and no 'they' came later. First there was a knowing beyond knowing that this one I call 'me' must walk out of this life. There was a knowing beyond knowing that it was not up to this 'me', this woman. It was what I must call a choice-less choice to leave everything I knew for something I knew not. But, quite naturally, the walking-out brought consequences. There was a home and family and friends and commitments. There were beings that I loved very deeply, beings for whom my attachment was strong. There was their pain, their loss, their grief at my leaving.

And so the first step into that third definition of madness began: the turning of one's back on intuition. The mind kicked with all its ferocity: guilt, responsibility, anger, grief, love, the seemingly unbearable heartbreak of having caused pain to another being, the heartbreak of leaving those I was profoundly attached to; but most of all fear. Fear of the unknown, fear of the known, fear of loss; fear that I was losing my mind, fear of not knowing anything any more. Fear that if my intuition was 'wrong' that I would wake up one day alone and desperately regretful of my calamitous misjudgement, and of having so badly hurt the people who loved me the most. But, Katherine, fear is a wily monkey. It knows precisely what it is doing. It blares at full volume so all can hear. And why? So that it may silence that little voice that knows. Now, if I say to you that no one wishes for other people's freedom, there is no judgement being made. None at all, for in fact, that is simply the mind's way. No mind wants to be free; no mind wants to discover that it is no-thing, for it is too busy with the business of being a thing, a person. When another being comes along and appears to be shedding all things personal its only reaction is to rise up and prevent it. And so the 'crazy' machine begins. And what debilitating labels it connives: depression, breakdown, despair, delusion, bipolar, schizophrenia, the list goes on.

But here lies the curious thing. In order to 'break through', as it were, it seems very often an apparent breakdown must take place in which everything we have formally understood is stripped bare. *Of course*, there is confusion! And there is anger at life for bringing what appears as such destruction; and tears. My goodness, Katherine, so many, it is no wonder they considered me broken. I was, thankfully, I was. Broken, distraught, grief-stricken. But grief-stricken for who, for *what*? Yes, my life; yes, my loved ones, but even more devastatingly, grief-stricken for the death of the one I loved the most – me, my mind, this one I knew as I. Which made me question, well *who* is grief-stricken? I had not the language then to articulate, but Heart knew. Heart always knew, despite the wily monkey, despite the despair that caught hold because, and only because, doubt was strong and momentarily convinced me my intuition was madness. It believed for a while, although never wholeheartedly, that I was all those labels, and so the machine kept turning, my own fear feeding its revolutions.

Can you see how such a one might end up in a place such as this? *All* human beings are deluded, Katherine, doctor to indigent. All minds, even those not locked up and medicated, are fraught, chaotic and delusional, until the realisation comes that we are that principle beyond the mind. Oh boy, that's the real revolution. That's an earthquake waiting to topple this world. And what do I mean by this world – this mind, this ego, this personality. Six billion worlds all believing that they are the fundamental truth can only lead to the devastation we see out there. But that is for a future conversation. What matters now is looking to your own earthquake, to the toppling of your own delusion. Trust me, this shall be the most benevolent self-destruction ever imagined. That all of this so-called journey – destruction to enlightenment – is also imagined we shall come to later. I do not wish to confuse you any more than perhaps I already have. For now, speaking relatively of 'my' own despair I can say I would not have it otherwise.

That we insist upon sedating and numbing the pain is a curious aspect of this play. Human beings are so terrified of the potential destruction that they will go to any lengths to prevent it. Why else prescribe mood stabilisers and so-called anti-psychotic medication? Why else pump the system with sedatives and tranquillisers? We cannot bear to watch another being's unravelling and so we pathologise and deaden. You would rather have me bent double with medicated lethargy, rather see me drooling and incoherent, my eyes unable to open, my muscles unable to support themselves, my words slurred and my body shaking with tremors, than face the truth of what we are. Better to anaesthetise than question; better to control and silence that which we do not understand. What an extraordinary act of sabotage and yet entirely understandable. It is true that awakening to the Reality of what you are is but the first step to freedom. Next comes what I describe as loving brutality. And this can be messy and noisy and emotional as Life pushes us to face each deception, as it scours us of all pre-conceptions, of all our notions. It washes us clean so that we may see with clear eyes, with pure, natural mind that this manifestation we call *us* is but a perfect mirror to Self. What I am saying is that even after Seeing has occurred there is the entire world to clean before we are free, and for some beings this means creating more delusion within the delusion, so afraid are they of their own Self. And yet – and here lies proof of the benevolence of Life – even the delusion within the delusion provides, if we choose to look, the key for our very own unlocking.

But as I have urged before, you cannot take my word for it. This must be your discovery. I am not trying to trick you or convince you or induct you into a set of beliefs. What is being pointed to is beyond belief. It is so simple and obvious you will laugh when you see it for yourself. Forget my words and discover for yourself. There is only one place to start and that is to ask what you know. If there was one thing that you could say that you know beyond anything, beyond refute, tell me, without imagining, without speculating, what would that be?

Oh wow! Look at that for timing! Saved by the bell of enquiry!

4

⚭

This room was a delight. Averi tightened the blanket around his shoulders and took in his surroundings for the first time. The right-hand side where he had lain on the divan was a wall of glass, much like the wall of his bedroom. But here the view was entirely of the sea. The table where he sat was in the corner by the open kitchen with its old-fashioned stove and great black pipe. From here he surveyed a living space of rich colour, of burgundy rugs and russet upholstery, of densely woven fabrics from far-off lands. It was like stepping into a children's storybook. Averi stepped away from the table and explored. There were carvings and murals and beautiful ceramics. Averi picked up an exquisitely turned ebony vase. Tiny crescent moons had been inlaid in creamy moonstone with such minute precision it seemed like the work of a miniature genius. There were maps, old-fashioned ones, with ships in seas and peoples on lands with fine calligraphy marking each territory. And here on the wall opposite the window was an enormous tapestry wall hanging. Averi leaned in close. The detail was mesmerising. There were peoples in strange garments from different ages; women in trailing gowns and elaborate headwear; men in animal skins; hunters and dancers, acrobats and kings; warriors and wise women and children playing jackstones; there were exotic animals and brightly coloured birds and peacocks and butterflies and fish; there were strange plants of every colour and variety; and in patches of blue were sewn dozens of sailing boats; their white sails full and expectant; their tiny sailor-men and sailor-women gorged on a feast of adventure through time. Averi ran his finger along the weave until it settled on a giant whale-fish.

- It wasn't a fish and it isn't a myth.

Averi turned his head. Nyx was sat with her legs curled under her on the sofa, her head leaning on her hand. How beautiful she was. Averi was so struck he was tongue-tied.

- They say it was a mammal that millions of years ago may have lived on land. The ancients called it the *record keeper.* It had seen and imbibed the journeys of countless life-forms, and in particular that of man. You have heard of their music, perhaps. It was said that some human beings were able to tune in to their frequencies, into the collective mind, and read the records of time. Such beings very often had no idea how they knew what they knew. Many did not awaken to their ability until the time came for their listening. But when they did they were able to intuit each facet of man's myriad journeys. They were in tune with the harmony of the universe, swimming with the wisdom of whale. It is a sad irony that our forebears did not honour this mighty creature, this being in the ocean of Existence. You look at me strangely, Averi. Do I shock you with my story?

Averi sat down on a stool beneath the tapestry. There was a severity to Nyx's words. That was what shocked him. She was not smiling in that playful way. Her stare was as sharp and unyielding as a spear.

- Do you know what it is that you are looking at?

Foolishly, Averi turned his head, but at this proximity all he saw was a blur of colour.

- Which aspect of the weave might you be?

Averi was confused.

- Aspect?

- Any clue yet?

- Nyx, I don't understand. If I am Nothing how can I be an aspect of *some*thing?

- Ah.

It felt suddenly as if all life had been drained from the room. With perfect synchronicity the light that had almost blinded Averi earlier now disappeared behind cloud, and the space fell dark. Nyx got up from the sofa, crossed to the slats and pulled them open. There were clouds all right. Thick and ready for a fight. Averi wondered if he had said something to upset her. What could have made Nyx turn her back to him as she refilled her coffee cup at the counter? She liked the cream and was pouring in plenty like a milkshake.

- Tell me about your Nothing, Averi.

Averi shook his head and held his breath. As he released he laughed.

- Was it wonderful?

- Oh God, Nyx, it was tremendous. I don't know what happened to me, but that fever must have burned me to the ground. It felt like the widest expanse of space. It all dropped away, but without me trying, you know.

Grace came and burst into my heart. It broke my heart wide open; that's the only way I can describe it. And the love that was felt was boundless. I *was* Love. I *am* Love. I saw it, Nyx. I saw the I Am that I Am. A knowing that I am not this body; that this body shall come and it shall go. That I am limitless, timeless space. The vibration, the hum of Existence was the very fibre of my being. And I feel so grateful – so goddamn grateful to be stripped of all my ideas. I am the hum of Existence itself, Nyx, I am Existence itself.

Nyx was looking down at her coffee cup, stirring in a teaspoon of sugar. Averi had to take several breaths to calm himself.

- Yes, I see that. But what knows this?

Averi stared, open-mouthed.

- There are two points here, Averi. And they are subtle, so I need you to pay attention. You are looking at me now as if I had punctured your life-raft.

- What I experienced, Nyx, is not a life-raft. You're always saying it must be my direct experience. Isn't that what you say?

- Sure.

- So, what do you want from me?

Averi was up from the stool.

- You should know the answer to that by now. All I ask is that you draw your attention to that sense of Existence in you.

- Isn't that what I've been describing?

- And discover what knows Beingness. – Averi?

- Don't talk to me.

Averi was pacing with his back to Nyx.

- Who is sulking right now?

- You call this sulking?

- What would you call it? Is it anger?

- You're damn right it's anger.
- Anger at what?
- At your smugness, that's what.
- And?
- And at your undermining my experience which *you* told me was mine to have.
- That's not what I said.
- Oh, really?
- Whose experience are you talking about?
- And now that I've had an experience of my own, fast as you like you're all over it. Oh no, that couldn't possibly be the *right* kind of experience. Oh, excuse me; I must have had the wrong kind!
- *Whose* experience?

Averi leaned his head against the tapestry and punched the wall. It hurt and his knuckles throbbed, but he was too upset to care. This was too much. Just when he had thought he and Nyx were finally on the same page, she had upped and changed the goalposts. There was no one else he could talk to about any of this. The boys would stare at him like a lunatic, if they didn't already. And now his one ally was turning on him; the only one who he *thought* understood. And on top of it his final recourse nowadays seemed always to be tears. It was revolting. Averi angrily wiped his eyes dry and leaned his back to the wall.

- I'm not trying to bully you, Averi, but I am going to puncture you, this raft, whatever has been built. What I want from you is everything you've got to give.

Averi laughed, bitterly.

- I think you took most of it already.
- I want what's left.
- You don't ask for much, do you?
- I want you to let me drown you.

Averi snorted his astonishment.

- Without a struggle.

- I'm happy to be your plaything, Nyx. But, on this occasion—

- It shall be a sweet drowning. Merciful, in fact.

- Uh huh.

- But not if you struggle.

Averi kicked his heel against the skirting board to then find he had met Nyx's gaze. He felt his chest rise and his chin wobble as he tried to contain himself.

- Please—

- *Whose* experience, Averi, are you talking about?

Averi wiped his face again.

- I don't know.

- You describe a beautiful moment of awakening to Truth. And what is discovered? Not just a feeling of spaciousness, but that you are spaciousness itself: you are emptiness, an expanse without boundary, a formless, timeless no-thing-ness, effulgent with love, with peace, with compassion. I told you there are two points here, most delicate, to observe. First, you must find out who was experiencing this moment.

Averi shook his head.

- What have we discovered before? Where does experience take place? Where, Averi? In your feet? In your liver? In your bones? *Where?*

- Alright, I get it. My mind!

- And who is the experiencer of the experience?

Averi held his head in both hands. If he didn't have air very soon he might explode.

- You know what I experience? That you get off on this little ride of riddles. Seriously, I'm done now. I'm *exhausted*!

- And the one feeling this resistance, who is this one? Identify yourself.

- Leave me alone. I just wanna be left alone.

Averi had made his way to the stove. He flicked open the coffee pot lid and looked inside the pot, but it was empty.

- You're asking me to leave you alone and you don't even know who this 'you' is. This one who is feeling anger, and confusion, and exasperation; this one who had the most amazing experience, who is he? Where do all these feelings and experiences reside?

Suddenly, filled with rage, Averi picked up the coffee pot and threw it across the room. It bounced off a wooden dresser and clattered noisily along the floorboards.

- In my mind! I've said that.

- And what feels a feeling and experiences an experience?

- The mind, okay, the mind! So, in other words, my experience of Self wasn't real. Isn't that what you're telling me?

- The answer to that will only confuse you right now. First you have to see, Averi, that the mind is not the big, bad enemy here. Only a mind that has identified itself with something causes suffering and delusion. Don't forget that you have manifested as a body and mind. The 'I' you describe as formless, undifferentiated space has manifested itself into differentiated form, into a person, an individual with its own unique characteristics. And this particular form in front of my own form comprises a male, five foot ten, strong stature, sarcastic wit, love of the ocean, etc. etc. etc.; all the things that comprise an Averi are unique to an Averi, but we know that they won't last. The trouble began the minute you were given the name Averi, for then you forgot that you were anything other than this name and your sex, your family, your country and everything we have described before. The point is this: the mind is not the bad wolf. Without a mind you would not be here in this form. You would not have the opportunity to *experience* Awareness. Yes, *experience* Awareness, Self, Beingness, *That*. There has to be a mind for this possibility.

But let us be clear about this mind. What exactly do we mean when we say 'mind'? In its most primary sense, Consciousness *is* Mind. We might call it Great, or Universal Mind. Within Universal Mind is born the individual mind of each manifest being. The individual mind – just like its parent – is of itself pure, natural, free. But with the arrival of the individual a very great dance is about to begin. This is the dance of 'I am other than you'; this is the dance of the *thinking* mind whose story is to become fully identified with being an individual. The thinking mind is not separate from natural mind: it is *all Mind*. It is merely an aspect of Mind that has come to believe so fully in its own autonomy that it has completely forgotten its original state. The human journey, then, is merely to remember our original state. We shall unravel this more as we go along, but for now what is important to see is that *natural mind* is the natural state of this human existence, for it is through natural mind that we may shine as a mirror to that which birthed us – Universal Mind, or Consciousness. This appears as the extraordinary gift that Consciousness has given itself, if it were capable of such things. For Consciousness cannot experience itself. And why not? Because what *Is* cannot see what *Is*; what is one with itself cannot see itself, do you understand? Can an eye see itself?

- No.

Averi leaned his elbows heavily on the central counter.

- No, of course not. It needs a mirror in front of it in order to see itself. And that is what this body and mind are. They are the mirror in which Consciousness may witness itself. Therefore, that which is seen in the mirror is what? What generally do we see in a mirror?

- A reflection.

- Exactly. A reflection. The mirror *and* the reflection are both phenomenal. I don't know if you are with me. But, Averi, whatever anger and impatience are coursing through this body, I urge you to let these words sink deeper. The mind is a mirror; a mirror to Self, to the Un-manifest principle of Awareness. When the mirror is clear the reflection is clear. In other words, when the mind is clear the reflection of Self is clear. But the human journey is to cloud the mirror with all sorts of story and interpretation. The mind, the mirror, forgets somehow what it is, and dives into its worldly condition – that of belief and thought and the intellect: into the cloudy story. It is not quite as simple as to say that we must destroy the thinking mind. Remember our conversation about that? For, in fact, it is through the shenanigans of the thinking mind that Awareness can become aware of itself. Oh boy, what an opportunity! This is the great gift to humanity. Who knows what other means of experiencing are being experienced by other species in the universe? What is clear for *this* manifestation is that the journey itself, ignorance to wisdom, is somehow wrapped up in what it is to be human. Imagine Consciousness as a diamond and each form as one facet. It may take many lifetimes for one facet of the diamond to wake up to itself.

- You believe we have many lifetimes?

- Remember, belief has nothing to do with anything real. Belief is speculation; it is a thought in the mind; one of those clouds. The reason we get so churned up with this question is because we are still so attached to being an individual. What you are really asking is, does Averi have many lifetimes? Of course, Averi doesn't. Averi is unique to this moment of cause and effect. And yet somehow the learning accrued in this being appears not to be lost in time. It remains within the collective mind and reappears in another shape and form to build on those learnings and most likely *un*-build those learnings. It seems somehow that the point is a joint accumulation of so-called learning.

- You mean like all the facets of the diamond have to wake up?

- Yes.

- But, you're speculating.

- On this point, yes, I am speculating. It is a mystery. And yet, at the same time a deep knowing sees that anything is possible in the play of Consciousness. What is seen intuitively is the *play* itself.

- The play?

- I asked you some moments ago to investigate what knows that sense of Beingness. Let us return for a minute to the mind. We said that the mind is for experiencing; the mind is the experience, the capacity for experience, and the one who experiences; all three aspects rolled into one. The confusion begins when the mind grabs hold of an experience and redefines itself by that. Remember we talked about the little boy who became thoroughly identified with his family history? He is so identified with being a boy named Averi, that pretty soon all events and so-called traumas become a part of his identification, until Averi and all his apparent psychology fill the mirror completely. Self remains reflected in the mirror, but all view of it is totally obliterated. The same is true even of our most spiritual of experiences. These too are at risk of being held up and held on to as a 'part of us'. How easy it is for us to adopt our new spiritual identity; and how subtly it takes us in. Remember, Averi, something is prior even to this most profound taste of the Unknown, *because it is still an experience*. We know that the taste, the capacity for taste and the taster are three aspects of the mind, and that this mind is the mirror to Self. In order for you to have tasted Self as you did, the mirror had to be cleared of all story so that the reflection could shine through with absolute clarity. The mind was purified of all identification. When the mind has renounced all attachment to ideas, thoughts, beliefs, memories, wants and needs, when it has seen through its own delusion, then it is clear. And what a view it now perceives! Just as you described: the timeless, formless, effortless space of Beingness whose very scent is the fragrance of Love. But – and this is a big but - you *must* be vigilant that your mind does not jump back on the desire train, and begin desiring a repeat of this experience. Can you see how subtle it is? The Impersonal is being wrapped up in a new personal identity. How quickly you shall become a person who has had a wonderful experience, who becomes fully attached to this experience and to the new person it appears to have made you. This is why you were so angry with me, because I attempted to strip you of your new spiritual identity; because I wished to divest you of ownership of your experience.

But, my beloved Averi, our next step and my second point is the final divestment. For do you not remember that I said the discovery of Truth is a veritable disenfranchisement? Is it not now seen that what is perceived is still *only a reflection*? Let me say that again: what is perceived through the mirror/mind is still *only a reflection*. Can you see how easy and subtle it is to make the reflection Absolute Truth, when in fact it is but a mirror's perception of Truth? Now perhaps we can answer your question as to whether or not your experience of Self was real. Now that we have seen that it is only a mirror image.

- Okay, wait a second.

Averi crossed from the kitchen counter to sit on the sofa opposite Nyx, pulling his legs up underneath him in the same way as she.

- Now it's just words?

- Yeah. I mean, how can I be sure that my sense of Self is just a reflection? I hear you but, I don't know, it just kinda sounds all poetic now.

Nyx laughed and nodded her head.

- It's good that we go slowly, and make sure nothing false gets past. Tell me now from your own investigation if your innate sense of Being can *see itself*?

- What, you mean with a pair of eyes?

Again, Nyx laughed.

- You tell me! We have already confirmed that Awareness itself is not active. The most we can say about it is that it is aware. It does not think or talk or learn or remember. Do you agree?

- Sure. But we do say that it watches.

- That's true. But let's look at this watcher. Is it passively or actively watching?

- You've asked me this before.

- Well, don't try and remember what you discovered then; discover *now*. When it watches is it making judgements based on its perceptions?

- I guess not.

- Don't guess. Look. Is it watching with intent or desire or wishing for any outcome?

- No, it doesn't want anything.

- Does it lean towards anything in particular?

- No.

- Does it have preference?

- No, it just watches.

- It just watches passively, we might say, then. And is this watcher – this space – able to see itself? You tell me it is capable of watching movement within it. But is it capable of watching its own self? If space is space without shape or form or end, if it is one with itself, is it by itself able to see itself? Look for this answer. Don't imagine.

Averi felt his spine soften into the cushion.

- What is happening, Nyx asked.

- My spine is relaxing.

- Okay, so relaxing of the body is happening. This too appears in your Awareness. Awareness Is and out of it arises the sensation of relaxing. Keep your attention on the Awareness itself. Let sensations and thoughts come and go as they please. Don't interfere with them. You remain as that silent Presence. Let us speak from there. And tell me what you know.

- Awareness is always there. It's as if there is Awareness and things move in front of it.

- For example?

- Well, that right now talking is taking place. And the seeing of you on the sofa opposite me is taking place. There's movement to the seeing and talking but the Awareness remains still.

- And who is this Awareness?

- Awareness is I.

- And can this 'I' see itself?

Averi could feel his mind bristle at this question.

- I get the concept, I think. I can see, like you said, that a physical eye can't see itself. But how have we made the leap from the sense of 'I' suddenly equating with a physical eye?

Nyx paused and looked at Averi sideways.

- Okay, the thinking mind is back again, sniffing about for answers. So let's keep stripping all the way back to the pure I Am. Not I am Averi or I am a man. Simply I Am, nothing more. Are we together?

- Yes.

- Is the I Am-ness divisible?

Averi blinked and looked.

- I can't say that it's divisible or indivisible. It just Is.

- It just Is. Does it stop and then become something else?

- I don't—

- Look and see. Does what Is turn into a different kind of what Is?

- Of course not. What Is is what Is. There's no change to it.

- So, if Beingness is unchanging and doesn't, so far as you can see, become anything else, then it must be eternally One with itself.

- Yes, One is One.

- One is not two?

Averi shook his head and smiled.

- You serious?

- Of course, I'm serious. This we must be certain of.

- Then, no, my sense of Beingness is merely that – Oneness. That is clear in me.

- So, now tell me. Can Oneness look outside of Oneness and see itself?

Averi felt his eyes soften.

- No, Oneness can know nothing of Oneness except through this mind.

- Except through this mind. Do you understand now why I asked whether One was two? Only through 'otherness', through 'two-ness', through me and 'you-ness', through *duality* is there the possibility for experience. Something must have occurred to Oneness. Only by dividing itself through the mirror of mind is Awareness now capable of recognising itself. An 'other' had to be born in order for Awareness to reflect itself back to itself. But we will return to the actual division later. For now I want you to see, Averi, what your own words are pointing to. How long we have been chastising this thing called mind when all along it is our angel. We had to wipe it clean first, knock it right out of its senses, before returning to witness its inherent purity. The mind has manifested seemingly to allow Consciousness a glimpse of itself. But this glimpse needs clarifying to avoid any future delusion. If mind is a mirror, then what is seen in the mirror is not the actuality, but a mirror image – a mirage, a facsimile, a hologram, a representation, a dream – whatever quantum mechanics or spiritual teachings want to call it. When you look in the mirror is your reflection made up of the same tissues and blood as your actual body?

- Of course not. It's just an image.

- And what is an image, but a ghost, a phantom, an *imaginary* form? Can you see now that in the truest sense your experience of Beingness is not real in any Absolute way? It is but a pure reflection of the Real. What a discovery! We have already seen that the thinking and feeling mind is not real in any profound sense because it is constantly changing. But now we have fallen deeper into the realisation that even our sense of Awareness is in itself unreal, because it is a mirror image of the Real. Nonetheless, a mirror does not lie. An image is always, as long as the mirror is clean, an accurate reflection of the Real. So now comes the question, what is this Reality beyond the mirror? There is one question you can ask that shall reveal Truth. This is the question I asked you earlier and which so angered you. *What is aware of your own Awareness?* Who is the watcher of the watcher?

At that moment, Averi's attention was drawn to the disturbance outside the window. A crowd of gulls were hurling their jabbing, metallic cries across the wind, circling and ready to dive. It was unearthly, somehow, with the clouds so injured, and the sea a grey wake. Averi turned back to see that Nyx had not moved one inch. She was staring straight at him seeing, he knew, how his attention had pulled him away. At once, Averi saw how fickle it was, this attention, how it settled where there was most diversion. It was like a greedy child in want of new toys. Too quickly new toys became old toys, and so the search began again. How utterly exhausting it seemed. Exhausting, unhappy and empty.

- Nyx?
- Yes, Averi?
- Can I ask you another question first?
- Of course.
- If the thinking mind is *always* jumping from this thought to that experience, if it's always hungry for more tasting, can it ever be free of wants?
- Do you remember we once said that to ask the mind to stop thinking is like asking the wind to stop blowing? Your own discovery is that the thinking mind is always hungry for tasting. So, as an effect in Consciousness, the doing mind and the 'doer' are forever on the lookout. And yet, here is the mystery: once we have seen through

the delusion, we somehow become more in tune with Universal Mind, or rather with our experience of Universal Mind. This experience comes via *natural mind*; that is to say, the mirror to Awareness, to our own Self, that shines through, unhindered, once the individual mind is no longer identified with being a person, no longer identified with the thinking mind. Thoughts may come, but they do not draw our attention unnecessarily. In fact, 'doing' is no longer thought-driven. All doing comes from the Heart. If doing is needed it is done, effortlessly, spontaneously, without the pushing of doership. But we'll come back to that—

- Wait a sec. I still don't really get what you mean by 'an effect'.

- An illusory phenomenon. That is to say, an object or a thing which is an illusion, a mirage; in fact, a dream within the dream.

Averi laughed and shook his head.

- Okay, wait—

- I know, bear with me. What do I mean by a dream within the dream? Well, let us look closely. We have already concluded that even natural mind is illusory, right? Somehow and some-why Consciousness has manifested a means to be a witness to its own self via natural mind and the various forms it shines through. Are we together on this bit?

- Yes.

- Good. This natural mind we have described as a mirror, as a lens that reflects Self back to Self so that it can see itself. But the image is of course not in itself real. No matter how perfect it appears, it is in the final analysis only a picture of the Real. This picture is therefore an illusion. But then comes along a further twist with the manifestation of a thinking and doing mind *within* natural mind. This doing mind is the changeable aspect, the mutable, inconstant, living and dying, beginning and ending aspect of cause and effect. Not only is it not real because, as we have seen before, something that is true must be ever permanent, but also because *it is still a part of the mirror.* It is the clouds on the mirror; it is the illusion within the illusion. Or to risk your wrath at my poetic terminology, it is the dream within the dream. Now can you tell me where suffering begins?

- In believing the dream to be real.

- And if both dream and dreamer are fundamentally unreal, is there any such thing as real suffering?

- No, it's just dream.

- It's just dream. But we humans believe this dream so ardently that we cannot separate dream from Reality. Quantum mechanics tells us that this whole universe is but a holographic projection. That the one is reflected in the many. Even science is using the same language to describe what you are discovering through your own enquiry. Enquiry takes us away from theory, however, away from speculation, and into the realm of intuitive seeing.

- But, Nyx—

Averi lifted his legs out from beneath him. He sat squarely on the sofa now and leaned his elbows onto his knees and his head on his hands as a great pulse of urgency bounded through him.

- There's something missing here.

- Tell me.

- If there is a reflector and a reflection and that which is being reflected, there still has to be something prior to all of this to know of its existence, real or imagined.

What a galaxy was spread in Nyx's face!

- And you said it yourself, Nyx, that every perception must have something prior to it in order that it may be perceived. There has to be a perceiver of even that which is being reflected, right? There has to be a perceiver of Consciousness itself.

Those dark orbs shone the entire universe.

- Yes, Averi. We have confirmed Consciousness as the watcher, the witness, the perceiver of all manifestation. So, who could this perceiver of the perceiver be? By asking this question you have gone beyond even Consciousness itself, to that out of which Consciousness was born. Some call it the Absolute. It is, in truth, nameless. It is the One prior even to Consciousness; the One out of which this entire universe and all its phenomena appeared. The asking of this last question negates all words; there is no verbal answer. What is there to know about Beingness? You said it yourself so exquisitely. You said you saw 'the I Am that I Am'. So, *who are you who sees the I Am that you Are*? Beloved Averi, do not conjure up a clever answer. This question shall silence all other questions. It leads you to Silence beyond silence. How perfect: the I Am that I Am. What else to say, other than your testimony is proof that even the sense of Beingness, the sense of Existence is seen from a deeper place; that, in fact, the sense of Beingness – the stripped I Am – is itself subtly phenomenal. You have gone beyond both object and subject, beyond 'I-me' and the 'I-Self' to that out of which 'I' emerged. I pushed you, Averi, because the wisdom revealed itself in your own words, but how quickly the mind jumped in to take possession of this wonderful experience. How quickly you were being defined by this new 'awakened you'.

- But does that mean I can't ever express joy at something experienced?

- How on earth do you jump to this conclusion after everything we have discovered? Of course you can express joy. You can feel any feeling you like, happiness, excitement, anticipation; even fear and anger may come. But none of them stay, and this you know. As long as you remain in recognition that you are that principle before any feeling or 'happening' which you experience, then you are free to experience all the colours of this manifold creation called Life. I'll say it again. Any phenomena can appear; any thought or feeling or experience. But what is silently, effortlessly witnessing all phenomena, even the most subtle of all phenomena? Don't wait for me to give you an easy answer. This is your recognition to be recognised. Who is watching all movement?

- I am.

- As what are you?

- I Am. Nothing more; just the space of Beingness.

- And what knows this? You said you saw the I Am that you Are. What are you that sees this? What is aware of your own Awareness?

Nyx smiled, and there was no answer.

Just Silence, beyond even any notion of silence. Slowly Averi sat straight. Inexpressible joy and the all-encompassing radiance of Love: this he saw reflected in her eye, this he saw as his own Self; neither separate nor un-separate; neither awake nor un-awake. And this Self itself was seen.

- If anger comes, does it touch You in any way?

- No.

- If enjoyment comes, might it be enjoyed without it having any effect on You?

- Anything can come.

- Anything can come.

Nyx reached into her pocket and pulled out a handkerchief. She wiped her eyes and blew her nose.

- There are moments, she said, when I wonder how it is that we are not all weeping for joy all the time.

And she smiled at her wonder as she shook her head.

- Blessed, Averi. Welcome home.

5

⚜

On Thursdays we tend to have fish of some description. Perhaps the chef has lost the will to create because we have had white fish pie for the last four weeks now. I'm hoping it's not the same one. It looks like everyone is thinking this, for the atmosphere in the dining room is wary and muted. Inmates are forking through lumpy potato as if prodding a dead specimen. All except Reynardo, that is. His ears may be on full alert, but he is quite capable of eating at the same time. Anastasia has just walked in again. Hairs prickle on the backs of necks; a collective intake has yet to release. Sarah lifts her head and scowls, her flecked cheeks pumping themselves up for a fight; Greg, whose guitar is leaning against his lap, puts down his fork and waits; Fat Nandi has spun on his chair, and is holding both his arms to his belly; even Silent Jane has lifted her head to watch; and Rose has begun to whimper. Her noise shall only feed this fire.

- Rose, I say. Please be quiet.

I am surprised at my words. They are firmer than I have ever heard myself speak. Rose shoves her fist into her mouth. Lydia is tightening beside me; her jaw muscles, her mouth muscles, her arm muscles; all are braced. Anastasia is behind us. She, too, is bolstered.

- Well?

Lydia slides her plate away from her. All eyes are upon it.

- I've told you, I'm vegetarian.

- Well, says Anastasia, stepping so close that I can feel her heat on my back. Lili is a vegetarian and she's not complaining.

- If Lili was a real vegetarian she wouldn't be eating fish pie.

- Anastasia, you can't force her.

Greg is almost hyperventilating. It has taken every ounce of his being to summon those words. But they are the floodgates to everyone else's.

- Yeah, Anastasia, shouts Reynardo over the deluge of complaint. Vegetarians do have rights, you know. You wouldn't force a Jew to eat pork or a Hindu to eat beef, would you?

- No one is forcing anyone to eat anything, Bill.

Reynardo goes purple at the sound of his real name. I don't think I have ever seen him so furious.

It is Sarah's turn next. She lifts her fork like an angry finger and jabs it to make her point.

- Would *you* want to eat over-cooked pasta every night of the week? Although looking at the size of you, you probably do. It seems to me you haven't given young Lydia much of a choice at all. I mean, look at her options, to bloat up like a heifer, or to go against a moral choice. If Lili wants to break her own rules that's her coffin, but I for one back the true martyr.

And she bangs the table with the end of her fork, again and again, inciting a whole army of fork bangers. I'm not sure everyone knows what they are banging for. But pent-up rage needs little encouragement. Anastasia shouts for quiet, but even her determined strength cannot match the drum of anger. Dmitri and another young nurse come charging into the dining room. But they, too, are at a loss. The inmates appear to be running this show and Lydia is its emcee. She picks up her glass of water, leans over my plate, and from a calculated height she slowly pours the contents into my fish pie. By the time of the last drop the bangers are too fascinated to continue. Lydia challenges me right in the eye. It is the cold lost stare of despair. I pick up my fork and contemplate the swill. Someone gasps as I slide my fork. And I hear Rose whimper as I eat.

I don't know why I did it. I know even less why she lets me stay beside her on the bed when in everyone else's eyes I have betrayed her. She hasn't told me what she thinks. Perhaps she is too angry. I didn't eat to spite her; strangely at the time it felt like loyalty. In truth, I didn't think at all. Did I rise to her bait? Why eat, when her argument was sound? And yet, at the same time these hysterics are so hurtful. Was I trying to burst that bubble? Honestly, I do not know. All I know is that I feel sick, sick to my gut. I look down to this girl-child beside me and keep the motion smooth and soft, stroking from the crown to the length of her hair. How unbearable it suddenly seems to see her unguarded; as if I were an intruder. Her lips have parted on a chasm of need. And I weep to know I cannot meet it.

I don't know what time it is, maybe two, perhaps three in the morning. For some reason I do not even think to look at the clock. Something has woken me; the same thing that pulls my dressing gown on, my socks and my slippers; the same thing that tiptoes me out of Lydia's room and into the hallway. The night lights in this place have that soft, foggy glow. They are concentrated around the nurses' desk, which leaves the hallway and living area in shadow. I like it, somehow. There is something strangely human about a psychiatric ward once relieved of its glare.

Suddenly, I stop, and instinctively move to the wall. Being caught breaking the rules, out of bed, and wandering the corridors in the early hours of the morning is not worth the trouble it will cause. Notes will be made, highlighted in my file, and it shall take months of dissection before I am free of it. A deep, back of the throat, grunting noise is coming in bursts from the nurses' desk. Giant John, the night warden, is asleep. I am amazed he does not wake himself up. It is then, in the tail of his out-breath, that I sense my watcher.

This is an image not easily forgotten. There is a flame from a lighter under her chin, and a ghostly corpse of a sparrow. I see now it is Reynardo's lighter, the yellow one he stole from the café. There she is, sitting in the corner chair of the TV area holding it over a magazine. A rosy, winsome bride beams up at me, chiffon of white veil and tulips the colour of damson. It looks cruel, her happiness, beneath this bird. If only they could both know the truth.

- Lydia?

- Stay away.

Her whisper is hoarse and it stops me. I sit on the armchair opposite, careful not to let the plastic creak.

- What do you want?
- I don't want anything.
- Liar.

The lighter goes out and she flicks it on again. Those grey depths are so empty, so desolate, they make me realise what little I know of this girl. And yet it does not matter. What I know is beyond details. How wrapped up she is in the business of suffering. It swathes her like a shield. To unpeel her would be to unpeel swaddling. She is right, I am a liar. I do want something very much.

- Lydia?
- Don't move.

Lydia is holding the flame to the corner of the magazine.

- You don't know anything, she hisses. You think you do. But you don't.
- It's true, I know nothing.

Lydia exhales, bitterly.

- You're such a liar.
- About what?
- That you even have to ask only proves how deluded you are.

I don't like to remind her that she is the one who thinks Special Forces are about to storm Saffron Ward.

- I'm gonna burn this place to the ground. It'll have been all your fault and you can't even see why.
- Do you know what I see?

Lydia shakes her head and scoffs.

- I see Love. I see unbound, limitless Love in the form of this one named Lydia. Do you remember when you told me what *you* saw? Do you remember your own words? My God, I could never have imagined such perfection to have come out of anyone's lips, and there they were, five words of Truth: the Love that I Am. Listen to me, Lydia. What you are is beyond these thoughts, beyond this fear, beyond whatever anxiety has brought you out into the night and led you down imagined alleyways. What you are is Freedom beyond even any idea of freedom. But you are so convinced that your mind is speaking truth that for you nothing exists but terror and rage and anxiety. That which is the witness to your anxiety, remain there. You said it yourself, you felt it yourself. Sweet, beloved Lydia, do you not realise that for five glorious seconds you dropped the world. You dropped the world and left existence to Existence. Trust that, forget everything else. This one, this person who wishes to wreak havoc and wage war, who is she? Who is she? Is she even a 'she'? Look and find out. Life has brought you to the edge for a reason. It has brought you to the edge to clean you of all false ideas about yourself; it wants you to recognise the Freedom that you are, Lydia. So it turns you upside down, inside out, it destroys in order to create. Can you not see the benevolence? Life is not here to hurt you, to wage war on you, or to aim fire at you; yet it is true it wants you to burn. But you must realise that only what is false shall burn. The real you can never be harmed. The real you is not a *thing* to be harmed or injured in any way. The real you is untouchable, unassailable. No one can hurt *You*. They may hurt your body; they may even hurt your mind, but how can the Love that you describe as the witness to your suffering ever be hurt? Look close and discover that it is without form, without shape, beyond time. It is no *thing* at all. Lydia, my love, you are That.

The giant has gone silent. The bird is staring straight at me, dispassionate and grave. I see its eye flicker to the desk to see if we are heard. It returns and I take it we are safe.

- Who is Nyx?

The lighter clicks shut and we are both now in shadow. It takes my heart a moment to adjust.

- You think I don't hear you when you're lying right beside me?

Lydia lays down the magazine and stands.

- You are kind, Lili, kind and good. But you're clever with those words, clever and manipulative; and someone has to tell you you're a liar.

6

Nyx stood up and crossed the floor to retrieve the coffee pot. Luckily the lid was still closed, so that remains were not scattered on the rug. She was scouring them out now into the sink, washing and rinsing, and then spooning in two fat tablespoons of fresh granules and filling the pot with water. Averi watched as she lit the gas ring, one part of his mind knowing it should have been him collecting what he had thrown, another part wondering how she could move. He felt locked in a vacuum of bliss.

- Now perhaps I can ask you, she said, which aspect of the weave you might be?

It took Averi several moments to register the question. Nyx turned her back to him while she washed out their mugs, but as soon as she returned to the stove, he knew that she was watching him.

- Have I thrown you?

Averi shook his head and laughed.

- I guess I should expect it by now.

- And?

- And what?

- Which aspect of the weave might you be?

- Well, I don't really understand the question, to be honest with you.

- Oh no?

- No!

They were both smiling. Nyx nodded as she opened up a glass cookie jar.

- Okay. Which part?

Now they laughed as Nyx laid out some cookies on a plate.

- Would it help if I asked you when you think you might be going back to the *Chariot*?

- *What?*

Averi felt both smile and humour drain from his face.

- I don't understand. How can you ask me that? I can't ever go back.

- I see. Do the boys know that?

- Of course not. I've barely seen them to tell them.

- Why can't you ever go back?

Averi opened his mouth, but couldn't articulate.

- *Because*.

- Because?

- *That* life is over.

Averi's words hung in the silence. He was so shocked that this situation wasn't plainly obvious, that he didn't know what else to say. Nyx leaned her hands on the counter, waiting for the water to boil, without offering anything. They waited without speaking for several minutes until steam began to lift the coffee pot lid. Averi watched Nyx pour two cups, one black for him, one creamy and sugary for herself. He should have stood up and offered to help, but somehow he felt rooted. Nyx did not appear to mind. She carried both coffee and cookies over to the low wooden table between the sofas and sat, curling her legs under as before, and wrapping a turquoise shawl about her shoulders. The colour was startling against her dark hair and brown skin, and for a moment she might have been a queen or a courtesan from another era.

- What life is that, Averi?

She leaned forward and picked up a cookie.

- Help yourself.

- You like to eat.

- Yeah, I like to eat. I like a lot of things. I like to bake – homemade – and she lifted the cookie, proudly. I like painting and making things. I like collecting, as you may have noticed. I like old world art and pottery. I like new world music, though I'm sadly not possessed of a musical bone. How about you?

- What about me?

- Tell me the things that you like.

- Nyx, come on!

- Why so shy all of a sudden? You forgotten the things you like; the things you're good at?

- Of course not.

- So?

- So, I like the sea, you know that.

- Why?

- I don't know why. I just kinda get it.

- Get what exactly?

- I dunno. Its rhythm, I guess; its moods, its secrets.

- Its secrets, huh?

- Yeah.

Averi picked up a cookie and broke it in half.

- Like what?

- I dunno. Like knowing which way the wind is gonna turn just by the smell; like knowing how long a swell will last; like knowing which tide is about to turn even when I'm way out on a catch.

- You can tell which tide it is when you're out to sea?

- Sure.

- That's amazing. There can't be too many people with that gift.

- Well, Averi shrugged, eating the cookie. I'm not sure it's useful for much.

- Does it need to be?

- Well, what's the point of being good at something if it doesn't get any reward?

- Oh, that. The reward.

Averi braced himself as Nyx sipped her coffee.

- So, you think nothing's worth doing without a reward?

Averi rubbed his face and grinned through his fingers.

- What?

- Come on, Nyx.

- Does a painter paint just for reward?

Averi stretched his arms up and behind him.

- Does a dancer dance just for praise?

- Okay, sure, but a fisherman fishes for fish. There ain't much point otherwise.

- Of course, and a dressmaker makes dresses and a farmer sows his fields. Whoever said they didn't? My question relates to the seeker of *reward*. Here is my challenge to you: do you suppose you could go on a catch and be free of all expectation?

- You mean go on a trawl and not mind if the nets come up empty?

- In essence.

- Well sure, if you don't mind going hungry; if you don't mind having the gas turned off because you can't pay your bill; if you don't mind losing the *Chariot* because you can't afford the upkeep when the rot sets in.

Nyx laughed, a honeyed and rich song that could not help but make Averi smile.

- You sure like to build a story.

- Well, what's your point?

- My point is you're not listening. Once again the mind is full steam ahead, both hands on the wheel, determined and desperate for control. Take your hands off.

- Off what?

- Off the wheel, Averi. Who's driving this bus?

- Oh, it's a bus, now.

- It can be whatever you want it to be. The point is you need to hand over steering.

- To *who*?

The minute it was asked, Averi fell silent. The answer mushroomed and squeezed him out of the room. Nyx lowered her eyes and cradled her coffee cup in her lap.

- Is that not what happened during the storm? You let go of the skipper and surrendered to the wave.

Averi swallowed.

- I don't know what happened.

- I think you do. Something trusted; even *beyond* trust, something inexplicable knew to let go and to allow the *Chariot* to be rolled. When you say you 'get' the ocean, what you really mean is that you become one with it. You no longer feel a separate entity. It is no longer 'you' and the 'ocean'. You listen and it is simply You. This You is then free to guide you. But do you see how quickly the mind takes over? With all manner of certainty and bravado; with ideas fixed and intractable. Then the rug is pulled out from under him and silence comes. And just a few seconds later, the thinking, doubting mind is back on your brow.

- 'Cos there are still questions, Nyx.

- It's good that there are. Let them all tumble out and use them to wash this one clean.

- So?

- So what?

- So, doesn't it seem kinda lazy and irresponsible to you? I mean you can't expect to just sit back and wait for life to give. That's just arrogant.

- Uh huh.

- And besides, all of us have a responsibility not only to ourselves, but to our families, to our communities, well, to the world even—

- A responsibility for what?

- How can you even ask that? To contribute; to do our bit; to provide so that we can pass something on. What, you want me to just hand it all over, hand over responsibility?

- Yes.

- That's ridiculous.

- Hand over your existence to Existence. Allow yourself to be completely *irresponsible*. Look at how the mind is up on its haunches! Such a thought! It's almost heresy. The very idea that we might not be responsible for our destinies is enough to incite world panic. It might almost be enough to have me lynched. For does this not describe the very core of who we think we are; the very core of our human rights – to be able to carve our lives as we see fit; to push and strive, and mould, and demand; to wish and dream and hope and pray. Is it not the widespread doctrine that we can be whatever we want to be? We're addicted to progress and achievement because we are addicted to the notion that we are at the forefront of shaping our lives. If that were stripped what on earth would be left? Who would we be without decision-making and planning and achievement and responsibility? But *this* one who feels so responsible for life and its outcome, identify him; this one who thinks he knows without doubt which is the best path, the best action, the 'right' thing to do, who is he? This one, Averi, is the real arrogance. This one lies at the core of a personal identity; this one is just a thought.

- Oh, so this one who fishes to make a profit so he can pay for his father to be in a care home, this one is just plain arrogant?

- That's not what I'm saying.

- Of course I have to strive. Without striving nothing happens.

- That's not true. That's an assumption. Find out first who is striving. Who is this doer? See how angry this makes you. We can spend weeks talking about Self and discovering Self; you can discover with absolute clarity the nature of Existence, and one mention of responsibility and the question of who exactly is in control of your life and you are up and shaking for a fight. The human mind so desperately wants to control. It wants to keep both hands firmly on the reins of this life, but what I am saying to you is simply to let go of the strings. Allow Life to live *you*. Words are playing a little here, because of course you *are* Life, but I say it to make the point. Let's investigate this doer, Averi. Together, right now, let us discover the nature of this doer.

- I'm tired, Nyx.

- I'm not surprised. A lifetime of doing is exhausting.

Averi put down his coffee cup, got up from the sofa and crossed to the window. It was cool on his forehead as he leaned on the glass, and refreshing. What a world was out there. Grey marl and white tips, a sky loaded with expectation. He would not know any of this unless he were here to see it. A tight zoom suddenly pulled Averi in on himself. He would not know any of this unless he were here to see it. No listening, no feeling, no sensing, no talking, no seeing, no experiencing without – without what? He was what? The zoom had pulled back until a laser was beaming inwards. His own awareness. Nothing was experienced without his awareness. And this awareness was constant; unchanging, silent and still. It was him. He was Awareness. Everything else, the whole wide spectrum of his experience occurred within that space of Awareness, of him-Self.

Averi turned and looked to Nyx.

- This is—

- The godly principle, yes, Averi.

Nyx was staring up at him as if she knew his entire being.

- Now tell me, she said, if the world exists without You.

Averi swallowed.

- Do you remember how angry you got with me that day on your terrace when I suggested that nothing exists without You? Without 'you', I said, there is nothing, there *is* no world. Do you remember what you replied?

- That if I died the world would still exist.

- And now? Where are you now? I have a feeling there is still very much an Averi in possession of this newly discovered 'awareness'. We need to root this one out. The godly principle you are discovering is not a unique principle set aside for one man.

Averi sat on the edge of the divan and looked at the scene outside.

- Have I confused you?

Averi stared without answering.

- What is happening in you right now?

- How is it, Averi asked, his eye fixed on the sea, that Awareness appears to come and go, when I know it is constant?

Nyx frowned and paused, as if she had been pulled from one train of thought and was now conceding another.

- That doesn't seem to make much sense. If it is constant it cannot come and go. Only your attention comes and goes. As I have said before, Averi, recognition of your innate Self is the first step. Next we may, from this new perspective, sweep Averi's layers clean. And be warned, these layers have layers within their layers, so dense is our conditioning. Just when we think we have peeled away one, another appears in our enquiry. Remember how easily the mind will take this new spiritual identity for its own and how quickly it brands for itself a new batch of delusions. What is required, Averi, is nothing less than absolute surrender, especially of this one who thinks he knows what to do with his life. Can you lie, hands at the feet of That, and abdicate all responsibility for your life?

Averi shook his head. All at once he could feel his pulse race and his breath rising in his chest. He stood up from the divan and started to pace.

- Let us imagine for one moment that you have no say in the outcome of your life; that you are devoid of all creative power. Strong stuff, huh?

- So, you're saying a man can't even have dreams?

- Sure he can have them. Just don't believe in them. More pertinent to ask is who is the dreamer? Let us say that even to try to determine outcomes, to strive and to wish and to will things into existence is pure arrogance. For who is this one striving and wishing and willing, Averi? And don't just give me the answer you think I want to hear. I want this to be your discovery. I want you to free yourself from the tyranny of dreams. For don't you see you're dreaming a dream within a dream. How much tighter do you want the knot to be?

- Nyx, wait a second! Can you not allow me this moment? I'm standing at the window and it comes like an arrow – the perception that every experience appears in my own Awareness. Don't you get it? Don't you get how extraordinary that was?

- Who must I allow that moment to?

Averi threw his hands up in the air and swore.

- What do you mean, *who*?

- *Who?* Are you now in possession of that extraordinary moment? Must I leave you to bask in this memory and call back later so I can finally cut off your head?

- Please, Nyx, if we're gonna talk, can we talk straight?

- Oh, this isn't straight enough for you? I'm talking about cutting off your head and that's not a clear enough image for you?

Averi turned on the spot, hands on his hips, and caught his breath.

- And while we're at it, what about the rest of the world that *isn't* your experience? Is that somehow separate from your Awareness?

Eyes to the floor, Averi sighed.

- Okay, we'll come back to that. Right now I want us to be clear about this one who thinks he's still in possession of a life. Do you remember that conversation we had on the beach when I asked you about the one who thinks he is responsible?

Averi felt hot tears again and had no means of stopping them. He turned so that Nyx couldn't see and wiped his eyes.

- Averi? Look at me. If it's any consolation it shall be a merciful chopping.

Averi laughed as he sniffed.

- Well, that's a comfort.

- I'm pushing you, Averi, precisely because you have recognised that you are Awareness itself. Can you not see the divine opportunity here? It is *because* this shift of perspective has taken place that you can begin to see the great play and all its detail with clear eyes. But we still have much to clear; the mirror is quick to refill its tarnish, and your attention is still quick to jump. There is no judgement; merely that we have some unlearning to do. But I need you to see that I could not be having this conversation so easily had you not come into recognition of your Real Nature. Dearest Averi, that is Grace itself. Grace in the recognition and Grace in the unfolding. Now, this one who feels a sense of responsibility, tell me again about him.

Averi took a deep breath and sat on the arm of the sofa. He could hear that patient smile as Nyx spoke.

- Are we together?

Averi nodded and, with childish reluctance, looked Nyx in the eye as she asked her next question.

- What do you mean by responsibility?

- What do *I* mean, or what does *it* mean?

- Speak from your understanding.

- Well—

Averi looked to the rug and contemplated the intricate swirl as he thought of what he understood. It seemed strange to pick apart a feeling that he thought he knew. It suddenly didn't seem so obvious.

- I guess it means wanting to do the right thing for myself and for other people. It means looking to the future, being prepared. It means doing things that you don't always want to do but doing them because they feel right.

- Such as?

- I don't know. Like listening to Patch go on about his dead moth collection and pretending I'm really into it, because I know he loves to share it with me. I dunno. And more serious things, like sticking with what you know because that's what you've always done and it brings the money in. That feels responsible.

- Why?

- What do you mean, 'why'? Because it's the right thing, it's the good thing.

- According to you?

- According to everybody, Nyx. Everybody has a sense of what's right. I don't think that's so complicated. What are you saying? That I shouldn't listen to Patch just because it bores me?

- Of course not.

- So, what then?

- All I am asking is to find out who is this one who feels responsible? Where do feelings arise?

Averi slapped his legs, impatiently, and slumped into the sofa.

- In the mind.

- To feel responsible is a thought arising in the mind, no?

- Sure. So?

- So, you tell me. I'm not spoon-feeding you anymore.

- Come on, Nyx, it's just not practical.

- Who is having the thought that he must be practical?

- I am. My mind is having the thought.

- And where does belief occur?

- In the mind.

- So *what* is doing the believing of the thought?

- The *mind* is.

- Don't be truculent with me. It doesn't wash. You think I'm sat here just for the heck of it? You think I'm spending all these hours with you just for a laugh? Look now and tell me what is your direct seeing with regards to this mind.

Averi bit the inside of his lip. There was nothing worse than to imagine he had upset Nyx. The sharpness of her words were a brand.

- I'm sorry.

- Don't be sorry. Just look.

- I know that there are countless thoughts and feelings and sensations. I know that they're constantly changing. I guess that is the mind's only consistency: that it's always changing.

- What knows this?

- I do. I'm further back somehow. Although that sounds as if I'm in some exact place, which I'm not. I'm not in any place. I'm not any*thing* to be in any place. I don't exactly know what I am, except that I can't touch what I am, or see myself, or smell myself, or taste myself. I'm just space, I guess, with no end to myself.

- If there is no end to yourself, are you separate from anything?

- … No.

- Are you separate from the Self expressed in form as Nyx?

- No.

- No. There is only one Self, indivisible and undifferentiated. And this seeing is made available through the form of Averi and his alignment with pure, natural mind. Now can you tell me about the one who feels responsible? Does Self itself feel any pull of responsibility?

- Self doesn't feel anything itself, but feelings arise within Self.

- Look at that! Self doesn't feel anything itself, but feelings arise within Self.

- But—

- *But?*

- How can I be sure that decisions and actions are right ones?

- Averi, there is no effort to discover goodness when you know who you are. Right action unfolds, simply and naturally, without you having to push for it. Somehow what is to be done becomes plainly obvious. But the doing occurs without you having to be the doer. Effort unfolds effortlessly. Do not imagine that the awakened being is somehow sat comatose in a pious corner incapable of any action. In fact, what is discovered is quite the opposite. And what a treat it is to discover! For how creatively this life unfolds! Without the mind's endless manipulation and coercion it is free to flow without impediment; free to flow the course that it is meant to flow. This is the subtle and beautiful discovery, that 'doing' may happen, and will happen; more to the point, it must happen, because we have manifested into the phenomenon of cause and effect. But, there is the implicit knowledge that the person is *not* the 'Doer'. Somehow, intuitively, we know what the right direction is, and thus become the instrument for doing, do you see? We may not quite know why we know what we know; sometimes only a part of the picture is revealed. But trust and a deep knowing that intuition is the only guide allows us to act fearlessly and truthfully. For no action that comes from Truth can ever harm another. This we have said before. Others may superficially wonder and raise the alarm; they may superficially be upset by our 'decision-making'. But this, in actuality, is not your concern.

Pay heed to these words, Averi, for they can easily be misunderstood and misinterpreted. Not for a moment am I saying that we act without care for others. Quite the contrary: the awakened mind intuitively acts from compassion. It cannot be otherwise, for consider this. What can be said with absolute surety is that pure Awareness is synonymous with peace, compassion and love. This is not just poetics, or some utopian ideal of heaven; we have not imagined some pretty thought or fairy-tale ending. This we have discovered through our own investigation to be constant and true. How it is true is not for us to know. This is the realm of the unknowable. But what is obvious is that if Awareness never leaves then compassion, peace and love can never 'leave'. What Is has no method of movement; it cannot come or go, begin or end. It simply Is. Therefore, out of this 'Is-ness' of love and compassion, deeds, actions and impulses appear. But, no matter their origin, not all deeds will be initially pleasing to others. Think of the boys and how hurt, even angered, they were at your not wanting to share this journey. It took them a while, it may yet still, but that does not make your isolation an unloving act. A deep knowing within you told you this journey was to be had alone, at least in the beginning, and you responded to that. You are not responsible for their feelings; to assume that you are is pure arrogance. For who knows what lessons they are learning in the process. It is true that in the beginning the mind is still struggling with itself and this muddies your behaviour. But the more you bring each facet of this personality under the microscope, and the deeper this one is scoured of all its associations, the purer shall your behaviour become. And to use your word, it is found that 'responsible' action, that is, behaviour not deliberately hurtful to others, occurs quite spontaneously.

What reveals itself is that without the burden of prior conditioning, all the daily activities continue as they have done, but this time freshly and freely. This play is thus free to play itself out, Averi. That is why I am pushing you to find out which aspect of the weave you are; to discover your part in the play. This way you can see both play and player with detached intimacy. I must tell you that there are some who say that the details of the personality don't matter, but we must be careful not to fall into an 'enlightenment trap'. We have to look at those details and know each idiosyncrasy. Otherwise they become the delusion within the delusion.

- The delusion within— ?

- Okay, first of all what do I mean by the details?

- You mean like all the tricks and stuff of the personality?

- Yes, but even more fundamental than that. What is your learning, Averi?

- I don't know what you mean – you mean this? This discovery of my own Self?

- I'm talking about the facet now; the details of the facet that is appearing in this moment of time in the form named Averi. Let us start from Self. We have discovered already that the body/mind is a mirror to pure Awareness. Without the body/mind there is no-*thing* capable of experiencing Oneness. You with me?

- I think so.

- Let's be sure. I need you on the same page here.

- Okay, wait. My discovery is that without Awareness there is no experiencing. Without Awareness there is nothing to know about feelings and thoughts and memories and ideas. Awareness is never changing, always present; whereas my thoughts and feelings come and go with the wind.

- And what provides this canvas for experiencing?

- My body and mind.

- Right. This very recognition reveals the possibility for Awareness to become aware of itself. But how does it do it?

- Through the mirror; through the mind.

- And didn't we already see that a reflection on a mirror is just a mirage? That this whole taste of Awareness is in fact a reflected image, a perception of the Real, a facsimile of the Real?

- Uh huh.

- And so tell me, Averi, what was our next discovery? If we are able to become aware of our own Awareness, of Consciousness, then there must be something prior even to Consciousness to know about it. Which says what about Consciousness? That it, too, is phenomenal; it too is very subtly dream. Oh my goodness, so the whole of Consciousness, both manifest and Un-manifest is seen from a deeper place. Just as you proved when you told me you were aware of the I Am that you Are. To wake up from this dream is to see the entire dream of Consciousness and all its unfolding play. But we'll come back to the play in a moment. I want us to return to those details.

Remember the mirror and its reflection now and consider for a minute the effect of this reflection. It seems judging by the number of beings and life-forms on this planet that something rather extraordinary has occurred to the reflection of Consciousness: it has split into billions of pieces, each piece a perfect representation of the whole. Do you remember we used the phrase the 'holographic universe'? What is a hologram but a projection of an image that through the process of reflection has divided into billions of pieces?

- But how, Nyx?

- I don't want you to get caught up in trying to understand mathematics. That is likely to pull you away from your own intuitive discovery. But, put as simply as possible, a holographic image can be produced by the splitting of a single beam of light into two. The first offshoot of light is bounced off an object – let us say our mirror – and the second offshoot of light is aligned to cross with the reflection of the first beam. The interference between actual light and reflected light causes a wave pattern. This wave pattern is recorded on film. When light is shone through the two-dimensional film, a three-dimensional image is produced – a hologram. Why am I befuddling you with physics? Not because you need to delve much further, only to see the significance of the holographic principle. Because, as you have perhaps seen, a hologram is essentially made up of millions of perfect self-representations. In other words, if a hologram is divided into one million pieces, each of those millions will be a perfect replica of the whole. This is the essential make-up of this entire physical universe. And each of us nearly seven billion humans is likewise a perfect representation of the whole. The whole is One. But the splitting is diversity.

Averi was in such deep concentration that it made him start to see Nyx get up. She shook off her turquoise shawl.

- Forgive me. I almost forgot.

She crossed to the kitchen, cut a slice of bread, slid open the glass door beside the divan and stepped out onto a narrow terrace. The moment she began to crumble the bread a whole family of starlings flocked to the ground and scouted for pickings. Averi watched as Nyx crouched and sprinkled those crumbs. He was stunned that one minute she could be dissecting the known universe and in the same breath pause to feed starlings. They were his favourites, though, with their buff-coloured spots like stars. How noisily they chattered, and it made Averi wonder who they were in this great scheme. If he as a human being were capable of being aware of his own Awareness, then what of the starling?

- I shouldn't encourage them, really, but—

Averi stared at Nyx as she slid shut the door and shook herself free of the cold.

- What is it?
- Is it only us?
- Only us what?
- Only us who have the capacity for Truth?

Nyx walked to the sink and poured herself a glass of water. She drank thirstily and raised the glass as an offer. Averi shook his head.

- The real answer to that question has nothing to do with capacity. They *are* Truth but in different form. But I know what you're asking. Does a bird know of its own Awareness? I have not manifested as a bird so I cannot truthfully answer that. It seems likely, however, that humans have been blessed with a divine gift; that all of creation in this known world has led to the moment of initial self-awareness in human beings. But this was only the beginning. In the early stages of human development, self-awareness conferred individual awareness of being a person; that is, recognition that 'I' am separate from 'you'. The next stage in our evolution is apparent, as you have discovered for yourself: to recognise that the person is but a temporary appearance within a deeper Awareness. But, and this is where we must pay closest attention, this does not make the person unimportant. The person and all its individuality bring us back to the great tapestry of Life. Can you not now see why I asked which aspect of the weave you understood yourself to be?

Averi turned his head and looked to the tapestry. From this distance he saw that there was a coherence to the images. They were not as random and arbitrary as he had at first thought. Up close it was impossible to see how one element linked to another, and in turn to another. But now it had taken form as a whole it was no longer just a colourful display of unconnected characters. It was extraordinary, impeccably wrought and precise, as if he were witness to—

- It's a story.

Averi jumped up on his knees.

- It's a goddamn story, Nyx! It's like … like witnessing the greatest story of all time.

Nyx was smiling at his excitement.

- And what's it telling?

- I don't know! I don't have a clue.

Nyx laughed, and waited. Averi saw her waiting as he slid back down into the sofa, as a thin chiffon dropped.

- Nyx?

- Yes, Averi?

- It's as if I were witness to the entire story of creation.

- And you are what exactly? Describe this witness.

- Just a seer.

- And this seer – can you touch it?

- No.

- Has it any discernible feature?

- No. Except that—

- Except?

- Except that it's like space. Just the space of Awareness. It's just a sense of Beingness, of Existence.

- And what knows this? What is aware of this Beingness?

Nyx was not smiling, but her eyes were the still pools of Love.

- I see that you have discovered the Beyond, the word-less-ness. From this perspective, Averi, we can now perceive with utmost clarity this entire manifestation. Even Consciousness itself is subtly perceived. Do you remember I once said I see everything with detached intimacy? From this perspective, my beloved Averi, the whole of existence within Existence plays out. I am in it, but am not of it. Each detail is seen, but I am not attached to it. And this is why I said to you, know your story, but don't believe in it. Your story is but one aspect of the great collective story, which is but an aspect of this Great Story of Consciousness. Can you see now why I say we must unravel the delusion within the delusion *within* the delusion? Or to put it more poetically, the story within the story within the story? You, the person, are one facet of the collective story, both illusions appearing within the most subtle of all illusions, the mirror of Consciousness.

The 'I-me' and the 'I-Self' both appear in what? In that which is name-less; that which is Beyond. So let us draw our attention to this facet named Averi, for this facet cannot be free until it is free of its identification with its own unique story.

Averi laughed as he exhaled. He leaned forward on his knees, and rested his head in his hands.

- How is it that you know all this?

- Who exactly is this knower, Averi? Who are you referring to?

- Oh, man!

Averi threw himself back into the sofa so low that he had almost slid out of sight.

- Let's stick with the facet. I don't wanna get more confused.

- You can sit there and tell me that you know *beyond knowing* that you are prior even to the I Am that you Are, and now you want to know how *I* know? We're not going anywhere until this knower is found and identified, Averi. Otherwise we may as well throw in the towel right now. And don't look at me with those big eyes as if this were a rebuke. Who exactly is this knower, and what exactly do we mean by knowledge? Okay, let's strip it back. Where does intellectual knowing take place?

- In the mind.

- And where is knowledge known?

- In the mind.

- We have already agreed that the thinking mind is far too inconstant to be trusted with real truth. So what might be said of the so-called knowledge contained there?

- That it's not true.

- If everything in the mind is subject to change, then it stands to reason that even knowledge is changeable.

Whatever is changeable is obviously impermanent. Since the definition of truth is that which is permanent and ever so, the knowledge of the mind cannot be truthful knowledge. So when the sages of old sought *Real knowledge*, what do you suppose they were indicating?

- Knowledge that didn't change, that wasn't of the mind.

- And what might that be? – Averi, if I said to you I know that I don't know, would you think me wise or the most ignorant of beings?

Averi laughed.

- Do I have to answer that?

- Truly. Nyx smiled. There is no wiser confession than to know I don't know. And why? Because it is an absolute abdication of being a knower. This is the greatest discovery possible for our human journey – that the one who thinks he knows is not fundamentally real, because 'he' is changeable. Self-investigation reveals that the knower is the thinking mind. The real 'I', the sense of Awareness innate to all human beings, is beyond both knower and knowledge. It is the space in which both knower and knowledge appear. In that sense *'true knowledge'* is not knowledge as we intellectually understand it. It in fact points to that which is beyond all knowledge – to essential Awareness. To 'know truth' is thus synonymous with being aware of one's own Awareness; to know no-thing is the most profound wisdom. This is intuitive knowing, Averi, not intellectual knowing, and here lies the great distinction.

- To 'know Nothing', then, is to recognise that I am the space prior to all things.

- Yes.

- Formless space that is no-thing.

- Yes.

- So, can I put my question this way? How is it that this knowing beyond knowing revealed itself to you?

- Grace, my beloved Averi. Just as Grace is revealing itself in you. *In* you, not 'to you', for, of course, you are not separate from Grace. It is simply that that which has forgotten is waking up to itself. It is as if Self calls out to Self and calls itself home. I have no answer as to why or how. Whatever I could say would only be supposition.

- But what *is* Grace exactly?

- What is it in you?

The question surprised Averi. He looked to Nyx, searching for an answer in those night stars. They were darker than all the galaxies rolled together. She blinked and her eyelashes whipped apart as if they were releasing a secret.

- Perhaps, she said, it is Love in action.

Averi swallowed against the burn in his throat. It seemed now true what Nyx said, that sometimes tears were the only gratitude for beauty. Somehow he did not want to shed them. They felt so intimate, so pure, he did not want to forget this moment. And then he saw how this thought alone blocked the purity of the moment.

- Can anything come, he asked.

- You mean any action?

- I mean in the mind. I still don't fully understand how I won't just become a blank of ... well, you know, without feelings or emotions or passions. I don't know that I wanna be without passion.

- This one who stopped for one moment and felt a feeling when I spoke about Grace. This one who tried not to cry at his own exquisite feeling. Tell me about him?

Averi looked to his knees. Even her voice was enough to break him.

- The one who tries to hold on to feelings, Averi, *this* one suffers. The mind that is unattached allows any feeling to come, so yes, in answer to your question, anything can come, so long as you don't hold on to it. Can you not feel the deep breath of freedom rush in? You can feel and sense any one of the entire universe of sensations. Some are even so subtle that there are no names for them, but you may experience them nonetheless. Anger may come, irritation may come; playfulness may come; the intellectual thinker may even come so long as he doesn't take over this ship. Thoughts and feelings are passengers. They have their passage and then they return from where they came.

- Which is where?

- You tell me.

Averi shook his head, unable to completely meet Nyx's eye.

- Where does everything emerge from? Whence does this entire universe and all its diversity appear?

- It emerges from me.

- And as what are you?

- I Am.

- And can you qualify this sense of I-Am-ness in any way?

- No, except that it just *Is*. A sense of Beingness; of no-thing-ness.

- And is this sense of no-thing-ness a blank?

- No. It's not even that.

- It's not even that. There would have to be something prior to blank to know about blank, would there not?

Nyx grinned her playful smile and leaned forward onto her knees.

- All that is knowable, all that moves throughout time and space, every concept, thought, action, creation, is born out of Nothing, dances in Nothing and returns to Nothing. It is all an appearance, dearest Averi. We are but dream dancing the harmony of Existence. You do not need to worry about passion. Passion will be felt, but you shall not be attached to being passionate; rage may come momentarily, but you shall not be so enraged; beauty shall be seen and joy experienced; but you shall not hold on to their qualities and fear their disappearance. For yours is the knowing that this ephemeral world must dance in your unchanging Silence.

Nyx reached across the table and took Averi's hands.

- And this Silence you have discovered to be the joy that never comes or goes; the beauty that is everlasting; the eternal bliss of Self.

That burn gave way now. Nyx held his hands as Averi cried. He pulled to be free, for it felt exposing to have his hands held away from his face. But Nyx held tight. These weren't the exquisite tears of gratitude; these were the tears of absolute surrender; the tears of release. There was no conscious decision to do either. Surrender came spontaneously and release followed. There was nothing else to do but to allow his body to spasm and shake; to allow the sobs to reach down into him and empty him out on the table; to be utterly willing and prostrate; to ask with profound humility for guidance. And still she held his hands, her head bowed, waiting patiently. When the sobs receded, the two of them sat together some time more; Averi's chest caught itself in that childish way; his breath calmed; until, so it seemed to him, nothing remained of his material being but a stretched and bleached canvas. His lungs took one last deep fill, and Nyx let him go.

He could look at her now. There was no smile, only Presence.

- Now, she said, we may begin.

Oh, *boy*!

Averi's eyebrows hit the ceiling. This was too much! This woman had stripped him, picked him, flayed him, broken him. There was nothing left but a bare carcass and now she was saying—

- We may *begin*?

Suddenly, Averi laughed. He laughed at the absurdity, at the wonder, at the sheer incongruity; he laughed because right now there seemed nothing to do but laugh, especially because Nyx had started too. Her shoulders were shaking as much as his. How unstoppable it was! That joyful, painful, irresistible laughter that rides on one wave and leapfrogs to another. Who knows how long they might sit in this state? Averi didn't! And if he thought he didn't know anything before, he knew even less now. Everything was up for grabs and quite frankly, Life could have it all. And just when they thought the surf was flat, a new pulse shot through and they were off again. It was delicious! At last, though, there was nothing left. Just like the tears the impulse exhausted itself. Nyx was wiping her eyes with a handkerchief, while Averi, slumping back into the sofa, wiped his on the back of his sleeve. He was so tired he felt he could sleep for a year, a beautiful sleep, empty and free. As he caught Nyx's eye he was about ready to tell her, but it seemed Nyx had no notion of sleep. She was pulling the turquoise shawl back around her shoulders, tucking her feet under her thighs and waiting as if for a response to a question. Averi grinned, turning his head in an expression of enquiry.

- Well, she said.

- Well what?

- This is the last question for today, I promise. And then perhaps we can take a walk.

- Oh yeah? Where to?

- I don't know yet. That depends.

Averi shook his head and laughed.

- God, that doesn't sound too good. Depends on what?

- On where you feel to go.

Averi smiled. To be with Nyx seemed to him to be in a permanent state of surprise. Whatever expectations he had were sure to wilt like cinder. Even now, he had assumed they would sit quietly, at least for a short while, so that he might enjoy this feeling of surrender. He laughed inwardly to see, just as she had said, how quickly his mind had jumped in and tried to hold on to his feeling.

- You asked an interesting question earlier, Nyx began. You said, 'If I am Nothing how can I be an aspect of *some*thing?' Let's look at that for a moment. It seems a pretty sensible thing to ask. But now maybe we can see our way through to an answer. In fact, your own testimony seems to be pointing a way. First of all, let us once again bring the attention back to that sense of Existence in you. Ferment in your own seeing. You said something beautiful earlier. You said that thoughts and feelings and experiencing emerged in you; that you were the backdrop to your own experience. Can you say a little more now, and not from memory, but from your own immediate seeing?

- Well, the sense of Existence has no beginning or end. It just Is. But when a thought comes it appears to have a beginning when it arrives and an ending when it disappears. Its coming and going doesn't affect

Awareness. Awareness remains while activity appears in front of it.

- Let us look a little more closely at this activity. Is it separate from you?

- I don't know what you mean.

- Is it completely unrelated to Awareness?

- Well—

- Look, Averi, don't think. At once those grey clouds of deciphering and trying to work it out appear on your brow. There is nothing to work out here. This is not an intellectual exercise. Draw your attention back inwards, turn that spotlight one hundred and eighty degrees around until it is burning its light *inwardly* in your heart, not outwardly in the world of ideas.

- Must I always be bringing my attention back?

- It seems that way in the beginning. For as long as the mind exerts a powerful pull, there has to be some effort to steer the focus away from thought activity and into Silence. This is only natural. But in time there shall be no effort required: seeing is seeing; there is no longer any required pause to stop and see. But don't worry about this, Averi. Trust that Life knows what it is doing. There is a perfection to this timing. Do not rush or push. All that is required is your earnest surrender to Truth and then let the seeing unfold itself in its own way. So, to return to the question: this thought activity that you are witnessing, is it separate from you? You say that it appears in front of you. Are you saying then that it is somehow an entity distinct from you?

- I don't know.

- So, look and find out. The answer cannot come from me. Open your eyes, Averi.

- But I can't focus unless they're shut.

- That's not true. Truth is not reliant on eyes shut or open. It is easy for sleepiness to come in when you close your eyes.

- But I do feel sleepy, Averi laughed.

- I know that you're tired. But I also know that the mind is looking to opt out of this question. I see how suddenly it wants to close in on itself in the easy oblivion of sleep. But be cautious of this, Averi. What is aware of this feeling of sleepiness?

At once it felt as if a veil had cleared his vision. How immediately clarity came when he ingested this question. There was no sleepiness, just the silence of Awareness.

- Look now, just as you are, eyes open, without any meditation appendages, and discover whether thought activity is a separate entity.

- I see that thoughts appear in my Awareness. And if—

Averi turned his head to the window. Outside on the terrace a raven was pecking at the remaining crumbs that had been left by the starlings. A raven! It looked up and held Averi's gaze.

- And if thoughts are appearing in me they must be a part of me. Any experience is perceived in my Awareness. I call it *my* experience because it's appearing within my Awareness.

- Is there any experience that can appear outside of your Awareness?

- Well, sure, if it's someone else's experience.

- Are you saying that someone else has their own unique Awareness?

- Well—

- Not so long ago you pointed out that my Awareness was not separate from your Awareness. If Awareness is without shape or form, if it is without beginning or end, then surely we cannot ever leapfrog into someone else's Awareness. Awareness Is. It is indivisible. Did you not see that Awareness was one with itself? That was how we discovered that Awareness cannot be aware of itself unless there is a mirror of sorts to project itself back to itself.

- So, in effect, you're saying that since all experience appears within the One Awareness, all occurrences are available to all of us. If there is only one Awareness, then all experience appears on the one mirror of Consciousness, which means any being can know of any experience that is appearing there, whether it's happening in their own visual seeing or not.

- You say that as if it were ridiculous.

- Not ridiculous, just—

- Is this your hypothesis or is this actual seeing? I don't think you realise the significance of your words, Averi. Ignore your mind's reaction to them. Let us really look closely at this one and let not one slip of deceit get through. Do you remember we talked about the holographic reflection that is comprised of numerous self-replications? The language of holograms brings us potentially into the realm of theory and hypothesis which does not interest us. But if we can discover that there is a parallel with the holographic principle and our own intuitive seeing, then the image may help give even greater clarity.

First of all, we seem to agree that Awareness is indivisible in itself. Intuitive seeing confirms that our innate sense of Being cannot be circumscribed. But remember, we confirmed earlier that this is what we might call an experience by proxy. What we are seeing is an image which of itself is not real. It is just a copy of the

Real. This copy is then split and reflected with perfect exactitude into many copies. Somehow the original image is split into us, into each facet, as we earlier described. Just like the hologram each facet is a microcosm of the macrocosm. Pure, undifferentiated Consciousness has reflected itself through this mirror, and in so doing has given rise to the many, to the entirety of creation, to the *individual being*, of which you and I comprise two. Do you remember earlier I said that differentiating is the means for experiencing? Through the splitting of the reflection of the One into the many, an 'I' and a 'you' were born. Consciousness had to create an 'other' in order to see itself, but in the process that 'other' somehow forgot its innate Self. It became wrapped up in the process of being an individual and a thinker of thoughts. However, now that remembering of Self is taking place we are, ironically, in danger of missing the truth about those thoughts. You said just now that thoughts appear within Awareness, which suggested to you that they were a part of you and not a separate entity. Is this seeing or surmising? Look at the thoughts that are arising within you right now and answer the question from there.

At that moment, Averi was drawn again to the raven. The thought had come that the raven, which was still pecking at the crumbs outside, had somehow come especially for him. A second thought arose that this was ridiculous. Averi discovered that he was able to stand back and look at these thoughts without judgement. He saw them as if they were two objects passing across his vision. He saw that they were somehow connected to him, but that at the same time he was the witness to them. He saw that he was both!

Nyx smiled.

- What is your discovery, she said.

- I see that I am both, Nyx. I can't separate them. There is thought and there is the witness to the thought and I am both. I'm not *fundamentally* my thoughts. They can only appear because I am there as pure Awareness to be aware of them. But still, I cannot say that thoughts are separate from me.

- And clarify again who this 'me' is you are referring to.

- Formless, limitless space. I am that which is present always, silent and still.

- So, would it be fair to say that thoughts and experiences are *aspects* within you?

- Yes.

- And if this 'you' is formless, limitless space that is present always, would it be fair to say that thoughts and experiences are aspects within space?

- Yes.

- And would it also be fair to say that these aspects, if they appear out of space within space, must in essence be made of the same stuff as space?

Averi stopped for a moment and stared. His staring took him through Nyx's pupils and out the other side. Thought and space were one and the same, how clear this was.

- Thought must be an aspect of Consciousness.

- Of course. Thought is Consciousness in form. You as a man are Consciousness in the form of a man; I am Consciousness in the form of a woman. Now tell me about the raven.

Averi was startled. He had not realised she too had noticed the bird.

- Is it possible he is somehow outside of the Consciousness field and is a separate entity? Or is he not Consciousness in form, only this time as a beautiful black raven?

Averi almost laughed as the seeing took root in him.

- Look at him, Averi, and tell me if he is separate from you?

Averi felt his eyes prick; it was almost too exquisite to bear. At once he remembered the seagull on the beach and how he had seen right through the body of the bird to Nyx behind it. What he had seen was indivisible, bird and Nyx, one and the same in essence; both forms essentially without substance, without solidity, essentially a holographic wave; both pure Consciousness in dream-form.

- You see how simple and obvious it is? Whatever sense you had about the raven can you now trust it?

Averi laughed and shook his head.

- I don't know. Some part of my mind just doesn't wanna believe it.

- Believe what?

- That maybe he's communicating with me.

- What might he be communicating?

- I don't know.

- Yes, you do. Look me in the eye and tell me what he is telling you.

Averi looked away from the raven and met Nyx.

- That it's true.

- What is true?

- That I am eternal. That I am not separate from any aspect of this creation. That I must jump wholeheartedly into the void, into the darkness of raven-space, into the Unknown. Only then I am free.

- Only then? Is this a future jump you describe? What of now?

Tears rolled and Averi wiped them away.

- Are you putting off your freedom for another day?

Averi laughed and Nyx shook her head.

- Pretty silly, huh? To imagine that this wonderful manifestation is not an aspect of You is the height of mind arrogance; it is the height of delusion. Everything that you see, everything that crosses the vista of your canvas is an aspect of You, of pure, boundless Awareness. But more than that, everything that has manifested – whether it is in your visual sight or not – is an aspect of You. For now that you have seen with clear sight that there is only one Self, one 'I', one Awareness, that your Awareness is not separate from my Awareness, that there is no 'I' and 'you' in any absolute sense, perhaps now you can answer the question. Does the world exist without You? When this question was first put to you, you thought I meant does the world exist without Averi, and of course you baulked. But now that you have discovered what 'You' are, that you are prior even to Averi, that you are undifferentiated Self, indivisible Awareness, that you are that principle in which Averi appears, how clear it suddenly is that the world *must* and can only appear *in You*. This form in the shape of Averi appears within You, as an aspect within You, indivisible from You. The personal 'you' appears within the Impersonal You. Just like the raven, the sea, the world.

From this deeper perspective it is seen with absolute clarity that if everything is Consciousness then nothing is random. It is seen that the raven as an aspect of You has come as a divine gift to urge your awakening. You may say, well what of the starlings, what of the gulls, are they not all giving me messages? Maybe they are, maybe they aren't. What matters is that some intuitive space in you listened and recognised *this* message in the form of raven. Life will strive to get your attention in any way that it can. In this moment of the play Self is communicating to Self via two forms: a bird and a man. How playful is this Existence that it can contrive so many ways to communicate with Itself. It is as if Consciousness is so delighted at finally being able to see Itself, it must dance with as many varieties of creation as possible. And somehow it brings into place all the means required so that one of its facets has a chance to reflect back a pure image. Raven wants you to discover Freedom *now*, not tomorrow. He wants you to see that you *are* Freedom. Freedom is not a place to reach or a goal to attain. It is not in any profound sense *attainable* because it is not some objective thing to achieve. All that is required is a wiping clean of that mirror, of the screen of Consciousness so that Self may witness itself without impediment. Can you see now why your question was so important? There are subtle layers here and I want you to be clear in your seeing. How can you be an aspect of some*thing*, you said. What is this thing?

- Awareness.

- Yes, but what have you discovered about Awareness? Tell me once again what you have discovered yourself to be.

- I'm just here, that sense of Being that doesn't have any shape or form. When I look I see that it's without end, and without border; that there is nothing I can see or touch; that I am—

Averi stopped. He saw suddenly what Nyx was driving at.

- I am no-thing. And yet ...

- Yes?

- To be an aspect suggests that there does have to be a something of which you are an aspect.

- And what was your deepest discovery made earlier today? You said that something was aware of the I Am. Your words were: the I Am that I Am. This suggests that there is an even deeper place of seeing from which even Consciousness is perceived. Awareness itself is being witnessed by a deeper Awareness. Are we together?

- Yeah.

- You sure?

- The I Am that I Am.

Averi heard his own words sink deep into his being. A thought came almost of marvel that such words had ever emerged from him.

- I am aware even of Awareness.

- Yes.

- I am prior even to Consciousness.

- Yes. And if that is the case, what might you be?

Averi settled in Nyx's eye.

- As we saw, so we see now: there are no words to describe what you are. You are beyond words. I see that you are free of the world in this recognition. You, Averi, have dropped from you. What space, what panoramic seeing, what expansiveness, and yet you are beyond even these distinctions. From this deeper seeing it is seen that even Consciousness, even Beingness itself is subtly phenomenal, is subtly objective, for it is witnessed as a phenomenon from a deeper Awareness. Therefore your question actually answers itself. You, the facet, are an aspect in some very subtle *thing* called Consciousness. From this deeper seeing *the entire play of Consciousness is seen*. Consciousness itself is a creation, an energy formed out of the Unknown. Now, so that we can be utterly clear, where are *you* in all this? The first stage of human self-awareness came with the understanding of 'I' as an individual. Here in front of me is the facet, the person, the one named Averi with all his thoughts, ideas, memories and experiences. The next stage is the recognition of a 'You prior to this you'. Guide me through.

Averi pulled his legs up and sat cross-legged on the sofa. He did not have to think; words just came.

- This 'I' is the Impersonal 'I'. It is the 'I' of Conscious Awareness. It is the non-doing space of no-thing-ness out of which all the events of the universe emerge. It is the impassive watcher of the personal 'I.'

- And then?

- This Impersonal 'I' is also seen. In fact, Nothing-ness is subtly something-ness. It's as if, Nyx, both the 'I-me' and the 'I-Self' are together swallowed up into a deeper Awareness.

- Exactly. Like I said before, both object and subject are seen. Many traditions speak of a divine three: now we can see them intuitively for ourselves: *the facet, the Self, the Unknown*. We have seen that although there is an appearance of many through the great mirror of Consciousness, what exists in truth is One; the one Truth, the Absolute, the wordless, the Unknown out of which Consciousness was born, out of which manifestation was born. Remember we said that what is one with itself cannot see itself. And so it was that somehow Unity created a means to reflect itself back to itself *via* Consciousness. It birthed an almighty explosion of possibility whose energetic display was Light itself: Unity therefore manifested as Light. And why should Unity choose light as its great infant? For what other reason than that light as we know is the means for reflection and refraction. And so the great holographic principle could unfold. Consciousness *is*

Light. But it is also the *means* for Light to reflect and create myriad offshoots of itself – hence the variety of manifestation. But remember, if Consciousness is the light-mirror through which Unity could project itself, Consciousness cannot be the ultimate Reality – *it is the means through which Reality may be seen.*

Now we may fully understand the implication and emergence of Duality. The moment Unity created apparent form in the shape of Consciousness, the immediate consequence was the creation of 'otherness': One had become Two; that is to say, Oneness had created some 'other' thing through which to reflect itself back to itself. This process occurred again as soon as Light reflected itself through the mirror of Consciousness and created holographic images of itself. These images, such as 'you' and 'me', *appear* as 'other' to Oneness and 'other' to each other. But remember, any 'other' is only a reflection – a mirage – of real Oneness. It has no substance – *no solidity* – of its own. Form is but an energetic wave-movement of coherent Light; it has only the *appearance* of substance. Do you see? Is this not what your own intuitive sight discovered? That the taste of Being is without shape, without form, without matter.

- No solidity?

- No solidity. Awareness, or Consciousness, is but an energetic, all-pervading force. The facets – or us – are but concentrated light energy: a product of original Light interacting with a reflected offshoot of light. We *are* Consciousness in heightened vibration. Human beings have their own unique vibration just as ravens, rocks, stars, butterflies have *their* unique vibration. But *all* are the same Consciousness-force; which of itself is what? *Consciousness is the mirror to Oneness, and we as manifest form are reflections of Oneness, which is the Real 'I' of Unity.* Once the facet is clear, a pure reflection of Unity is projected through the entirety of Consciousness. Just imagine the potential within Consciousness if all the facets were clear. Have we not seen and experienced that a profound rise in vibration occurs within the awakened being – that the hum of Existence itself throbs and pulses to greater intensity? Quite literally our own vibration intensifies; Light energy vibrates at a higher frequency. And what is its inherent quality? Nothing but Love, Peace and Compassion. Do not imagine you ever have to *try* being loving, peaceful or compassionate. For these emerge effortlessly when you know who you Are. Thus, it is seen that the great display we call Life is but an interacting dance of light waves reflecting, as we have said, the Real 'I' of Unity, the original Heart of Love.

Nyx reached for her water. She finished what was left, put down her glass and sat, silent. Averi stared, as if dumbfounded. He watched as Nyx unwound her legs and hugged her knees to her chest. He could not help it: a great geyser-sigh exhaled from his lungs. It rippled his chest and sucked in his stomach, much like a tsunami before it cries.

- And now that we have cleared up the nature of Existence we may come full circle.

Averi laughed as he choked.

- Full circle?

- Where do you suppose we are being led?

Those glints were shining so playfully that Averi could not help but be led by them.

- I can't imagine there's any place left to go.

- Perhaps you can tell me now which aspect of the weave you might be.

Averi threw his head back into the sofa.

- Oh, man! You're like a dog with a bone.

- It's one hell of a bone!

- But how can any of that be relevant after what you've just said?

- Because, if we ignore the finer details of Averi, we ignore the finer details within Existence.

Nyx sat grinning her challenge across the coffee table.

- You want some water? I want some water.

- Sure, Averi shrugged. Why not?

- Sometimes the fire burns so strong you have to remember to quench it.

Nyx got up from the sofa and reached for a glass from the shelf above the sink. As she reached, her sweater lifted and Averi spied a tattoo in the small of her back. It was a small crescent moon with a cluster of stars around it. The minute she turned and caught his eye, Averi felt embarrassed, as if he had given himself away. He knew that she saw his confusion but not a flicker of it showed in her face. She returned with the water and Averi drank, thirstily.

- From where you are sat what do you see?

Averi was not quite sure straight away what she meant. Nyx lifted her glass in the direction of the tapestry. Averi did as she bid him and looked to the wall hanging.

- Thousands of stitches, she said. One picture. And what was it you saw before?

- A story. The picture is a story.

- Of what?

- Of life.

- What makes you say that?

- Well, I'm not exactly sure of all the details, but from this distance I can see that some kind of a story is being told.

- Uh huh. Anything else?

- I get the analogy, if that's what you're leading to.

- Oh, you do?

- It's not exactly complicated, is it? The picture is life and all the characters within the picture are the aspects of life.

- I see.

- Don't look at me like that.

- Like what?

- Like I've just given you the lamest answer in the universe.

- I wouldn't say lame. But I would ask why the resistance.

- What resistance?

- To knowing which aspect of the story you are.

Averi exhaled as he ran his fingers up and down the creases of his forehead.

- Because.

Nyx waited.

- Because, what about free will?

- What about it?

- Come on, Nyx. It's like saying everything is pre-written. Like, I'm just a slot in the great drama without any say, or any power, to find what I want out of life. Like, you're a fisherman; stay a fisherman!

- Who wants?

- Okay—

- *Who wants something out of life?*

Averi took a deep breath.

- It's good if this pushes your buttons. Let anger come up, let resistance resist. You stay focused on that silent witness to all feelings. Reside there in your innate sense of Being. I know that you're trying desperately not to squirm right now. It's okay. So squirm! Better out than in. Let's allow these feelings to really air themselves.

- I just don't see how my role in life can be so neatly circumscribed.

- Who's speaking right now? Identify yourself.

- I don't know.

- Don't fall asleep, Averi. You want to close your eyes on your own Awakening? Is that what you want? I'll ask you again. Who is speaking to me right now?

- Anger is speaking to you right now.

- Anger is what?

- It's a feeling.

- And where do feelings reside?

- In the body, in the mind.

- And what knows this? What sees all feelings as they come, effortlessly and silently, but doesn't itself feel?

- Me.

- And as what are you?

- Just space. The space of Awareness.

- Okay. I know this is repetitive. But see how quickly the feeling of anger drew all your attention. While it was present, you could see nothing but anger. It managed to obliterate your entire sense of Self. Self, itself, cannot be obliterated, but the lack of recognition gives the appearance of obliteration. Now I ask, is it possible for anger to appear and for you to remain untouched by it? And look, Averi. Don't give me the answer you think I want to hear. What is happening now?

- Nothing is happening. There's a sense of Beingness.

- Has anger gone?

- No, it's still here.

- Is it as strong?

- No.

- Would I be correct in saying that anger is appearing right now in your Awareness?

- Yes.

- But by virtue of your recognition of that which is prior to anger, you somehow feel less swamped by the emotion.

- Yeah.

- So, is it possible for anger to appear and for you to remain untouched by it?

- Yeah.

- This untouchable one, does it have any wants? Look and see; don't imagine.

- I don't think so.

- Look and see; don't think. The formless, name-less space of Awareness, does it have the capacity to want?

- It doesn't have the capacity to do anything; it just Is.

- Is it lacking in any way?

- No. But there is a sense of lack.

- Who feels this lack?

- My mind.

- So, again, that which is aware of mind and all its movement, is it itself lacking?

- No.

- Who feels want?

- Averi feels want.

- And the one who wants to get the best out of life. Identify him.

- He's just a thought.

- *He's* just a thought. Not only is the wanting a thought, but Averi himself is just a thought. Wow, what a discovery! This you have in fact pointed to before. I wonder if you remember. And here it arises again; your own seeing. What is aware of this manifestation called Averi?

- I am.

- And as what are you?

- I Am; nothing more.

- And does the I Am-ness feel it wants to get the best out of life?

- The I Am-ness doesn't feel anything. It's just here as space.

- Is Awareness planning and hoping and reaching and trying?

- No.

- Is Awareness anxious to succeed?

- No.

- So who is this one who thinks he has free will?

Averi smiled and shook his head.

- My mind.

- How does it feel to be free of the burden of free will?

Averi laughed.

- I do feel lighter.

- Is there any concern now about responsibility?

- It comes up. But it doesn't bite so hard I guess.

- Do you see now what arrogance is contained within the concepts of free will and responsibility? They are an abdication of trust. The mind assumes it is in charge of its own destiny. But in the assumption a great cloud appears and blocks all view of your actual path. What is meant for this one is sabotaged by desire and want and manipulation. What a paradox that by relinquishing all desire and want Life is then free to be as creative as it can be. The deeper you sink into your own intuitive knowing, the clearer one's path becomes. There is no need to seek or figure out, or push for outcomes.

Whatever is this one's gift and doing shall reveal itself to the purified mind. Once the mirror is clear and Self has a pure reflection of itself, somehow Life is free. Having stepped out of your own way, as it were, you find yourself flowing in the river of Life as opposed to fighting your way upstream. I said earlier to trust that Life knows what it is doing. But you, of course, *are* Life. We have moved even beyond trust now. What has effortlessly occurred is a profound surrender to Existence, and an intuitive knowing that Existence knows exactly what it is doing. And who are you in all this? You are the 'surrenderer', the surrendering, the one who has been surrendered to and the Awareness even of that. This is self surrendering to Self. You surrendering to You; mind at the feet of That. Can you prostrate yourself at the feet of Existence and hand yourself over? Can you dive head first off the cliff into the dark Unknown?

 - There is fear.

 - Yes, fear comes. Fear of what, can you say?

 - Fear of— Fear of not knowing.

 - What greater fear can there be? The human mind seeks to know. To know is to think we hold the reins of this Existence; to know is to think we can control our world. But this is our great delusion. The human mind cannot hold the reins of the Unknown. It cannot control the Unknown, but it shall try to its last breath to maintain absolute autonomy of this kingdom called a person. What I am saying to you is to let go of the reins, to let go of the controls. Be willing to free-fall; be willing to *not* know.

 - How do I know that I will be caught?

 - Need I answer that? Who asks that question?

 - Fear asks.

 - Fear has come to challenge you to jump, Averi.

- But isn't fear a thought which is fundamentally unreal?

- Okay. I am now going to throw a potential spanner in the works of everything we have so far discussed and say *that what you are is neither real nor unreal; neither dual nor non-dual; neither awake nor un-awake.* Can you remind me of our previous discovery about the facet that is Averi?

- What do you mean? That he's the changeable aspect of Consciousness?

- Do you remember we asked if 'you the facet' is separate from 'you the Awareness'? Can we look again and be clear of our answer. The manifest aspect of Consciousness is what?

- It's me, the man called Averi.

- And the Un-manifest—

- Is the space of Awareness, of Beingness, that has no shape or form.

- But are they not, as we have seen, both Consciousness?

Averi felt as if the room had suddenly sprouted ears and was listening with the intensity of love.

- Yes. They are both Consciousness.

- So, are they in any profound sense separate from one another?

- No.

- If fear arises can it be anything other than Consciousness in the shape of fear? So far we have labelled feelings and emotions and experiences as part of the unreal, changeable aspect of Self. I now want to strip away these words. They are of immense help in getting you to recognise that you are not merely a repository of thoughts. But now I want us to look even deeper. Fear appears just as the raven appeared – an effect in Consciousness, an effect in You. You are thus appearing and moving in countless forms. It just so happens that this particular facet named Averi has a unique set of learnings to help him awaken to Self, just like all the other billions of facets throughout time and space. Each being has his or her own set of identifications that he or she must rake through and see through if they are to discover the Happiness that they are. Some psychological tendencies are with you from birth, prior to any parental or social influence; the rest are formed throughout the passage of lifetime. Some are so ingrained that it takes a laser beam to search them out. These identifications form the entire story of who we *think* we are.

- But wouldn't this be a very boring existence if we were all wiped clean of our individuality?

- That's *not* what I'm saying. Individuality is not a problem to be effaced. My goodness, quite the contrary. Individuality is Consciousness's means of experiencing itself: through the many the One is seen. This is crucial for you to understand and this is my point: that *only by cleaning yourself of all obstruction may your individuality truly shine*. Remember I said before, it is not the mind that must be eradicated, for the mind is the vehicle for tasting. Only *identification* with the *thinking* mind, with being an individual, causes problems. Before this inner earthquake began for you did you ever question whether or not you were Averi?

- Of course not.

- Was not Averi and all his thoughts and memories and experiences perceived to be the very core of your existence?

- He had to be. I couldn't very well say that Patch or Trindar were the core of my existence.

- See, even now, when the question is asked, your answer is still looking to the material individual for confirmation. Your mind says, well, I wasn't Patch and I wasn't Trindar. They are them and I am me. It keeps you firmly in the belief that you are first and foremost a person, clearly distinct from other persons. And because this is strong everything that is personal becomes your only reality. That day in your kitchen when you watched the ladybird cross your chopping board, you told me it was the first time that you became aware of the movement of your own thoughts. This is equivalent to a great mallet to the back of the head. Do you remember when you described to me that morning down by the harbour? You said you felt as if movement was happening by itself and that you were just the watcher of it, that there was an expansive, panoramic view all of a sudden. You were not only watching yourself, but you were becoming aware of the Self that watches. Listen closely and see the subtlety in that. You were witnessing not only your body and the movement of your mind, but you were also witnessing your Self as the perceiver. So perception was not just of the activity, but of the *perception* of activity occurring within this body/mind. Am I losing you?

    - Kind of.

    - Who is this perceiver of perception?

    - Well, me, I guess.

    - Which 'me' are we talking about?

    - The formless, panoramic 'Me'.

    - Okay. So, now let's take a step back. What was being revealed to you was that pure Awareness was prior to you the person. That everything you knew to be Averi and perceived from the perception of Averi occurred within your own Awareness. But, even this Awareness was *seen*. This is precisely what you confirmed earlier, that there has to be a perceiver of the perceiver.

- This might sound crazy, after everything we've said, but how is that recognition of any use in helping me to know what kind of a life I'm supposed to lead?

- Okay, let us get there, step by step. First of all, *recognise*, and then let's see if that question has any relevance. The 'I Am that I Am'. Talk me through again.

- Oh, Nyx.

- I know.

Averi was struggling. He stood and stretched himself. His body was aching, his limbs were stiff and his back was tight.

- I just—

- I know what you're going to say. But we're on to something here, Averi. I don't want to stop now when such recognition is bouncing in the air. There is no effort required. This is not about deciphering and trying to work anything out. All I ask is that you draw your attention to that sense of Existence in you. Is it tiring in any way? If I ask you to draw your attention to the tip of your nose, somehow you just do it, right? Easy, without exertion. I ask you to draw your attention to the big toe on your left foot. Do you struggle to get there?

Averi shook his head.

- No, of course not. How easily you can draw your attention to the body. Now see if you can likewise effortlessly draw your attention to that sense of Existence innate to you. Good. Now, have you anything to say about this sense of Existence?

- That I don't really know what it is. It just Is.

- Anything more?

- That it's like, I don't know, like space.

- Do you see how fresh this discovery is? Each time you draw your focus inward, it's like seeing a child witnessing something for the first time. Such innocence; such purity. Everything drops from you. Your opinions, your fears, your judgements appear to have evaporated. There is no need to try and stop thoughts. Thoughts can come in any shape or form. Any experience can come, Averi. I am not trying to whitewash you of all feeling, only your *attachment* to feeling. Remain purely as I Am. In time you shall not need to draw your attention into Self so consciously. It shall simply be the clear position from which the entire universe is perceived. Now, what more can you say about the I Am?

Averi picked up the blanket from the back of the sofa, wrapped it around him and crossed to the wood burner.

- Can I put another one in?

- Of course.

Averi took a log from the pile in the basket, opened the burner door and threw it in. As he crouched he looked at the flames that had sunk low. The heat on his face was a balm.

- What more can you say about the I Am?

- That it, too, is seen. The sense of Beingness is also perceived. Something is earlier than I Am.

- What is?

- *I* am. I am that which is aware even of Beingness, even of Consciousness.

- What you are, are you real or unreal?

- Neither. There are no distinctions. There are no words for what I am beyond the I Am.

- A feeling of fear – is it real or unreal?

- Neither. It's an appearance within me.

- And does this recognition help you to understand what you should '*do*' with your life'?

- This doer is just the person.

- Let's look at that more closely. Who thinks about doing something?

- The mind.

- Exactly. Now let us remember what discoveries we made about the mind. First, the mind is our canvas for experiencing. Without a body and a mind there would be no possibility for experience. So, the mind is not our enemy. The mind is our gift to our own Self; a means for Self to witness its own self. Remember we described the mind as a mirror to Self. Once the glass is clear, a pure and untrammelled reflection is seen. The mind is then free to experience its own Awareness. But, what gets in the way of this pure seeing?

- Thoughts.

- No, *not thoughts*. The identification and absolute belief of thoughts is what gets in the way of pure seeing. This you *must* be clear about. As I have said, any thought can come, and as you have discovered, even one as strong as anger could appear without it having any effect on *You*. A thought is only as powerful as your belief in it. Yes? Remember the suffering when you considered your belief as the only reality? The world of Averi was a world of strong personal identity, which is comprised of belief. Strip belief away, strip identity away, and what is left?

- Peace.

- And is this peace a feeling that makes you feel momentarily peaceful, or is it beyond any feeling?

- I don't know. It feels like a feeling of peace.

- And what knows even this feeling then? – There you go. You drop from yourself into absolute rest. Beyond even any concept of rest; and yet we use these words to give our expression to the wordless. Now tell me, what happens within Peace, within Rest?

Averi smiled. It seemed all of a sudden as if he were witnessing a vast vista of colour and movement. As if manifest Life were literally on a stage before him.

- It's as if this 'me' were a character on a stage and I were watching him play his part. There are other characters all playing their parts. There is the scenery, and there is the stage, and there is even an audience. I can see it all. There are exits and entrances, and billions of stories within the one story.

- The one story is what?

- It is Consciousness itself.

- And the billions?

- They are the countless facets of manifestation.

- And do you remember what we said about these facets? That each is a perfect representation of the whole. That via splitting its own reflection through the Consciousness mirror, Unity not only manifested in numerous unique and individual forms, but that each individual was fundamentally a perfect replica of Itself. Now that you are discovering you are the witness to the Consciousness story and to all those numerous reflections, what can you say about the actions of those reflections? If they are born out of Unity, can they be in any way random, separate or coincidental?

- Honestly, I wanna say that they're all connected, but at this moment I can't say it for sure.

- But you do say they are all a part of a story which is viewed from a deeper perspective?

- Yeah.

- I think you're getting caught up in whether everything is destined or not. Whether it is or it isn't, is not relevant to this conversation. Perhaps if I ask this question instead: does it appear to you that the actions of the person are important?

- Honestly, Nyx, I don't know.

- So, let's help you to know. Seen now as an appearance in Consciousness, recognising your position as that principle prior to both appearance and Consciousness, tell me of the actions of this person named Averi who is now witnessed from a deeper vantage point.

- Well, I can only speak from my experience.

- Of course. Anything else would be speculation.

- Well, there feels a rightness to being here, to having this conversation. There feels a rightness in the decision not to spend time with the boys. No question arises as to whether or not I should be here. I'm not looking for another experience to replace this one.

- Why not?

- Because this is right for now. Before the storm the only time I didn't question was when I was on board the *Chariot*. Off the boat I'd be wishing for some other scenario.

- Such as?

- I don't know. Like, if I was having a beer with Patch there was a sense that I was somehow missing out on some other experience somewhere else. Like, whatever was happening in the moment was never enough. I was always waiting I guess.

- For what?

- I don't know. For something to happen, something to fill that gap.

- And now?

- And now – I'm not waiting. There is no gap.

- Do you need anything?

- No.

- Do you want anything?

- Only Truth.

- Even this most spiritual of wants can now be relinquished. You *are* Truth. Is there anything lacking?

- No.

- And so the one who made decisions, and sought to do the right thing, the one who hoped and dreamed and pushed for outcomes – where is he?

Averi smiled. For a moment he was too choked to speak.

- Is Beingness pushing or hoping?

- No.

- No. With this shift of perspective somehow the mind is utterly cleared of the desire for outcome. For we have posed the ultimate question: w*ho* is this seeker that so desperately looks outside of his-Self to find happiness? A deeper wisdom reveals that desire keeps one forever chasing imagined futures and locked in a state of dissatisfaction. In a profound sense desire is not the problem. *Attachment* to desire is what causes so much trouble. This is a subtle distinction. From the perspective of undifferentiated Awareness what feels right for body and mind may express itself momentarily as a wish to do or act. Doing occurs, there may even be attainment, but there is no holding on to a desire of imagined gain. Happiness does not lie at the end of desire. It is a painful delusion to reach outward for something we suppose to give us happiness. *Happiness is Presence, it is our own nature*; doing for doing's own sake occurs within the happiness of Being itself.

How easy it is for the mind to take hold of a subtle distinction and build a story. Desire has become the so-called 'baddie' of humanity. It is a 'baddie' only so far as we hold on to it. Here is the paradox: relinquishment of all desire allows an appearance of desire to play its momentary part. Could it really be possible that one can be profoundly without desire and yet experience desire for another person, or experience an inner compulsion to paint a picture, or a sudden urge to climb a mountain? This is the journey of inner discovery. Philosophers and theologians have tussled so arduously *against* their inner desires, but have so rarely asked the question *who is the desirer?* This, quite simply, would have put an end to such tussling.

We might even equate desire with man's determined stance that he is in possession of free will. Here is the great paradox. To know without doubt that it is not up to the thinking mind, that one is not the great architect of one's own life, is to allow one's material path absolute freedom. Your aspect of the weave, Averi, is not yours to sew. But once we have renounced intention, extraordinarily, it becomes beautifully obvious how and where to place your needle. Does that make any sense? Can you begin to see how in the most profound sense the role that is yours *matters* because it is not separate from Absolute Truth? The manifest and the Un-manifest are one and the same. But the role that is yours to play can only become clear when the mirror is clear. Once clear of our mental obstructions, Life can flow.

- Do you mean then that there is a pattern to everything?

- What I am saying is that everything is Consciousness. And if everything is Consciousness which is trying to reflect itself back to Itself, then every appearance is pointing to this same reflection. The raven, the storm, the ladybird, Patch and the boys, me, you, this house, this island. Every perceivable thing is a reflection of Self, which in turn is a reflection of Unity. We know that if it is a reflection it has no actual substance. It is a mirage, a dream, a story. But the story is the key to understanding ourselves. Do you not see the irony? *Through understanding the complexity of the dream we fully awaken to that which is beyond dream.* Our individual stories, which you said are a part of the One Story, appear to have manifested for perhaps only this reason: to allow Unity to experience itself via the One Self-mirror of Consciousness. If that is the case it matters very much that the delicate psychology of each being is purified, aligned if you like, to Self. And that means *knowing* ourselves. To know the Impersonal Self, paradoxically, we must also truly know the individual self that has manifested as a person with a personality. And that means Awakening to Self is but the first step. Next must come a ruthless scouring-out of all delusion. So for clarity's sake, we must look to the personality, for it is here that our path out of delusion shall take its final and completed steps.

I said to you earlier that I am not your therapist. It is true I am not. I told you that for good reason – so that we might first rake the coals clear and break through to Self. If we had remained stuck in your personal psychology then we would never have made the discoveries we have made. Do you see? Only now from the perspective of the Absolute, from that prior even to Self, are we ready to face the task of seeing all the facets of this personality, of laying bare all the components that are working hard to keep you firmly locked in as a personality. Some traits are obvious, but some are so subtle that they remain unconscious. By allowing them to be brought into the enquiry and to be seen within the clear air of compassion and integrity, slowly those elements of your psyche that have caused pain and suffering are let loose of their chains. Then the unique facet that is the personality is free to unfold, beautifully and effortlessly. We cannot push this disenfranchisement, but we can remain in

Silence, with an open and earnest heart for Truth. How humbling it is to see through the layers of our own self-deception. This is why I have brought us back several times to this question – to what aspect of the weave you might be. To know your own aspect is to sink ever deeper into your own Innocence, into the Love that you are.

Do not forget that to witness the I Am that you Are is to witness the *whole* story, not just the aspect in the form of you. This does not mean that Averi necessarily knows all the details of all the aspects, only that the wide expanse is seen, the whole tapestry. You are no longer locked in the single stitch of single identity, so close to the weave that you cannot see beyond the next one. From this perspective distinctions of real or unreal are meaningless. All is One in myriad form. From Oneness the entire play is seen, even if, as you yourself said, you cannot entirely read it. For it is seen from this greater vantage point that one individual's learning is not separate from another, nor that an event can ever be lost.

Do you remember our discussion about the whale and how Native peoples considered him the repository of all that has happened in the story of this manifestation called Earth? However relative and unlikely this sounds, remember this is a story and anything can manifest in the play of Consciousness. It is merely the story within the story reminding us that everything is Consciousness in form. What was he said to embody? He was said to know of all human paths and their so-called journeys. He was a symbol of man's ability to recognise that which is true. He was the Natives' symbol of man's innate intuition, which once recognised is the wisdom of Being *and* of the relative path. To see what you are *beyond* manifestation is to see what your path is *in* manifestation. They are not separate. How can they be when Self and mind are both Consciousness? This aspect of the weave that is Averi is unique to this moment of cause and effect. And yet somehow, as I said before, the learning accrued in this being appears not to be lost in time. Learning seems to accumulate and is remembered so as to be built on and refined. It now becomes obvious that from the position of the Absolute, which is the Seer of all, a purified facet such as an Averi is able to see all apparent happenings throughout the history of time. It is no longer ridiculous to state that man is capable of looking into the past, present and future dream of all beings. This must be so since he is but Consciousness in form. Once the mirror to Self is clear, everything may be seen with clarity. But one being's clarity is not enough. In the end, perhaps all facets must be clear in order that the mirror is entirely clear, in order that Unity can see a pure image of itself.

- Are you saying, then, that we can have several lives, and that it may take several lives to wake up to the truth of our Existence?

- I have no answer to that question. This you must intuit for yourself.

- But, Nyx, when I was delirious I did see things: other peoples, other times, other lives, I think. It was as if I was surfing through time and remembering other bodies I've lived in.

- All I can say, Averi, is that Consciousness has the whole of creation at its fingertips and, without doubt, no limit to its creativity. Make of that what you will. What is evident is that a shift is taking place in Consciousness. Beings are awakening to their undying nature. And Consciousness is manifesting in whatever way it needs to in order to get our attention. How clear it is now from this deeper place that everything is a part of the great play. Knowing it is a play and that we are the actors within it means that one does not take it, or indeed ourselves, so seriously. And yet, at the same time, as a detached observer, one intuitively knows what is right.

There is a great tendency in thought to imagine that we 'can be whatever we want to be'. It lies up there with the great fallacy of free will and desire. In fact, we cannot be whatever the mind wants us to be. I would love to be a concert pianist, but that gift is not appropriate to this one. Not because it is impossible, for all possibilities are available in Consciousness, but because intuitively it is seen that this is not my journey. As a child I longed to be an astronaut, but if that were my path I should have been born with the requisite gifts. And Life would have somehow shifted itself to accommodate those gifts. This is a subtle distinction. For, of course, everything is known to the Self. But in the surrender to Self it is seen what is appropriate for each being. That is not to say that we are all doing the will of Existence. As I say, first you must surrender your own will to discover what is yours in this life. And you will see there is not as much available to you as you might think.

- You mean there's not much choice in what I can do?

- It's not about you making a choice among choices, Averi. How clearly it felt to you that all actions since the storm have been right actions. You do not even question them or wish them otherwise. And why? Because the movement has come from Self. Somehow Self has propelled you forward these last weeks and action has taken place. Doing has taken place intuitively and therefore effortlessly. Can you even say that at any moment you wondered what the right thing to do might be?

- I guess not. It just sort of happened. But it won't always be so clear. Ideas and thoughts are gonna come. How can I tell what is intuitive knowing, and what is my mind trying to work things out?

- Recollect the raven.

- The *raven*?

- You had some intuition about that raven, did you not?

Averi had to stop to remember.

- Well—

He looked at Nyx sideways.

- Tell me.

- Oh God, I don't remember.

- Yes, you do.

Averi laughed, but Nyx was serious.

- Well, first I thought that he'd come especially for me. And then I thought that that was ridiculous.

- Okay. Can you describe any difference in those two thoughts? Either in how they appeared, or in the feeling or atmosphere surrounding them.

Averi stared at Nyx and at once knew what she was pointing to.

- Actually, yeah. There was a difference. The first feeling came so fast that I didn't think before I thought it, if you know what I mean. It was deeper, or kinda like *behind* other thoughts, somehow. Does that sound crazy?

- And the second?

- The second was louder and more in front.

- In front?

- Yeah, like a loud shout in the ear instead of a whisper.

- And which do you trust?

How beautifully she peeled away questions to arrive at discovery. Averi smiled.

- I trust the first: the one which told me the raven had come for me.

- Uh huh. And what do you now make of the second?

- That my mind kicked in with a flat denial of my intuitive knowing.

- Because?

- Because it's scared.

- Of what?

- Of what it doesn't know.

- Can you see now how clear it becomes? There is no longer even any need to *decipher* between intuitive knowing and the thinking mind. Somehow their energy gives off a smell, an atmosphere, and you can sense at once which is to be trusted. Intuition is not a thought process. It is a knowing beyond knowing. Intuition comes without noise or smell or back story; without expectation or need. It is pure, effortless, still and silent. Intuitive knowing is, as you perfectly described, almost 'behind' thought; which is why it requires a refined ear in order to hear it. We must learn to tune in to its frequency and to listen to the wisdom of Silence itself. You noticed that when your attention was quickly drawn away from your intuitive knowing, the ensuing thoughts were noisy and blaring. There is a movement to thought, an energy that sucks us in and pumps us up. Thoughts tell you what you should do with your life and all the ways in which you should go about it. But of course this wondering about Life prevents you from being present in Life; prevents the recognition that you *are* Life in form, and obliterates the obvious: that Life knows quite precisely what it is doing.

At that moment, the log in the wood burner shifted and dropped. Its heady cedar smell filled the room, tickling the muscles at the back of Averi's eyes. He looked at Nyx and was surprised to find that she was not looking at him. Instead her eyes had shut. It was not the repose of sleep, though; rather the repose of Silence. Averi remembered how she had once turned to him as he leaned across the counter at the Boat Shop and said, 'We shall meet when you no longer need me'. How long ago that felt now. An age away, a whole person away, an entire universe away. For the first time he understood why he had once so craved to be with her. She had reflected his own Self back to himself. Such love he had seen in her, such beauty; but his mind had interpreted it and built a story. It was nothing to do with romance or desire, but how he had wanted both. Now when he looked he saw—

Just as he looked, Nyx opened her eyes. He saw Nothing. Averi did not know he could smile so wide. There was no 'she'; no person at all; just Love; formless, timeless, boundless Love; and this Averi knew to be true. The hum of Existence was one with this Seeing. And then the searchlight turned to the hum itself. Inwardly he asked, what is this that is aware even of a sense of Beingness? No words came to meet him, for Averi knew that he was Unknown.

7

It is only just becoming clear why Katherine and I were forced to postpone our conversation. How precious, how precise, how perfect is Life in our protection. A whole week has gone by since my train of explanation, since that Friday when Katherine sought me out; during which another world has crumbled, dealt a divine blow. Now Katherine is looking at me, across the interview table, her eyes tasting something new.

- You seem different today, she says.

I am suddenly too full to speak.

- Have you slept at all?

I shake my head.

- Has something happened?

Tears are falling, even as I smile. I don't know how to answer.

- It's not sadness, I reassure her. Only joy. To see how Life protects us.

- You think that the fire alarm going off is somehow connected to us?

The fire bell rang last week just as I had asked Katherine that first question. It was not a pre-organised drill, although it probably should have been. It's funny to think of our escape. Twelve psychiatric patients in various grades of panic and nonchalance, being pushed like a herd of sheep down three flights of stairs and down into the quad. When I saw Lydia last night with that lighter I wondered if she had set it off. But it doesn't matter who or how. I know that Katherine and I were not meant to continue that day.

- You really believe—
- I don't believe in anything.
- So, what then?

Katherine Kolinsky is sitting in my old chair. I look to this being and see how delicately trust unfolds. My voice wobbles in reply.

- Sometimes, Katherine, the only way to understand is to listen in the abstract, to listen in between the words, to feel their poetic resonance. How often it is that a literal translation denies all the colours within Existence. Why would you want to limit your vision?

- What is your vision, then, of the fire bell?

- My answer to that right now would raise a wall between us. The only way to avoid the wall is to make it your vision. What I can say is that Lydia is right.

- Lydia? What has she to do with it?

Wow, these tears are amazing. They have to come. I see Katherine's concern as I start to sob. I feel as if I had been laid on a slab, my heart palpitating and raw. I even feel my voice is different somehow: its tone, its slant, its vibration. The only way I can describe this feeling is as if I had been punctured in both lungs. There are no edges left. And it's beautiful.

Katherine leans across and hands me a tissue. I blow my nose and dry my face.

- Why Lydia? Because, I explain, another deception has been sliced through. And what a benevolent scythe she is. I know. You look at me without the slightest comprehension of my words. It's okay. It's better that I speak and risk confusion so that we can lay it all on the table and then work our way towards understanding. That you are here is auspicious enough. That I am seeing through my mind's subtle game is enough. Someone had to tell me, Lydia said, and I can't tell you how grateful I am that she did. She said I was a liar and she was right. This is how subtly delusions are built. My mind had taken hold of my own Seeing and so desperately wanted to share it. The beauty that I see, the love that I feel, fed a new identity – the one with an urgent wish to help. All mind, all ego, all arrogance. Real Wisdom cannot be contained by the mind, but how quickly the mind rushes in to cage it. In my case, and as I've said before, words and their beauty have been my trap; that and the mind's desire to save and to heal the hurt of this world, as *you* have before told *me*. Are we not each other's teachers?

Awakening is just the first step. Then, and only then, can the personality be put under the microscope with *real* understanding; it is then that the divine dissection begins. All the threads that comprise this Lili can now be unravelled. And how clear it is that this unravelling shall continue until there is no one left to unravel. The question that pulls the first thread is the question that came before the fire bell. But, Life wouldn't let us explore together until the subtle veil of the helper had been seen through, until the one who was *playing* the helper was punctured. Do you see? The question can come now, purely, without any specifics of intent.

If there was one thing that you could say that you know beyond anything, beyond refute, without imagining, without speculating, what would that be?

Katherine is looking at me with the wide gaze of the listener. I feel myself smile, a smile that reaches into the back of me and goes beyond.

- I don't know, she replies. I suppose – that I'm alive.

- Is it a belief?

- No. I know that I am.

- You don't *believe* that you exist, you *know* that you exist. So, let's remain there in the realm of intuitive knowing. Everything else is speculation and untrue.

Outside the door a fox is trying to get my attention. He is lifting his wrist up, pointing to his watch, and miming eating with both hands. Lunchtime has come but there is no impetus to move. I shake my head as subtly as I can and the fox blows me a kiss. There can be no other distraction, for this cornflower is coming into bloom.

- What is evident is that you know that you Are. But the real question you long to answer is 'as *what* am I'? Do you follow?

- I don't know.

- You know that you exist, this you have confirmed. But can you tell me with the same intuitive knowing what exactly you exist as?

Katherine sits as still and pure as a china doll. A crease then comes to the bridge of her nose.

- It's okay, I say. There's no need to think. Don't try to imagine an answer. This we can unfurl right now. Close your eyes and draw your attention inward to that intuitive sense of Existence in you. If thoughts come, don't try to stop them. Let them play in front of you, but pay them no attention. You continue to draw your attention inward to that intuitive sense of Being. Is there anything you can say about it?

Katherine opens her eyes.

- I don't understand.

- What is aware of this feeling of not understanding?

- I don't—

- It's okay. Keep your focus on that intimate sense of Being. Just Being. Can you do that?

- Yes.

She closes her eyes again and I feel her settle like space.

- That sense of Existence, just that sense of I Am. Does the sense of Existence have any form that you can see?

- No.

- Can you touch it?

- No.

- Does it have a shape?

- No.

- Is it male or female?

A few seconds go by.

- Neither.

- Does it have a beginning?

- I can't see one.

- Does it have an end?

- I don't think so.

- Is it limited to the bounds of your body?

A few more seconds go by.

- No.

- What else can be said about it?

- It's like space.

- Like space. The limitless, formless, space of Awareness. And where are you?

Katherine opens her eyes again, wide as prayer.

- I don't understand.

- Are you separate from this sense of Existence, this space of Awareness?

Katherine looks at me as if I had given her the moon.

- I don't—

- What could you be? This sense of shapeless, boundless, body-less space? You said you know that you exist. You describe Existence as formless, and without beginning or ending. So Awareness is who?

- It's *me*.

What a hum is this Existence! A world has slipped from her shoulders. What a smile of Perfection, of the Love that she is! My tears are falling, copious and sweet.

- Welcome Home, beloved Katherine, welcome Home.

EPILOGUE

1

A weak sun was struggling to get through. Those expectant clouds had brought snow in the last hour. The island was already a blanched tableau. It was stark and refreshing, with its bitter charge of silence in the air. Averi turned the corner and stood on the mount. On a clear day you could see across to St John's and Newfoundland. Today the sea spread out before him like slate. She winked where the sun caught her but otherwise remained still. Until, that is, a rumpus of gulls flocked in for lunch. Nyx walked to Averi's side and looked down to watch the fray that had gathered at the smell of a catch. To the right side of the jetty lay the *Chariot*. And there, backs bent to the haul of fish, were his boys.

Averi looked to Nyx, who smiled.

- Careful here, he said.

The slope to the harbour was steep and could be dangerous when, as now, snow began to harden. Just as he was warning her, Nyx slipped and yelped.

- Whoa, he said, catching her arm and steadying her. See what I mean?

- I think I'd better hold on, if you don't mind.

And she laughed that rich tone that bellied on the air.

The snow concentrated their attention and they picked their steps carefully in silence. Nyx was the first to speak.

- May I ask you, Averi, about Waldo and Hap?

Averi felt a twinge clamp shut in his gut. There was a bench halfway down the slope. He guided Nyx towards it so that he could sit. Anxiety had risen so sharply, he almost felt sick. Nyx sat beside him, seeming to know. He felt the heat of her, a warm presence of patience. She waited for him to look at her, but the minute he did he was forced to look away.

- So much fear, huh?

Averi nodded.

- I don't know why. They're not even real.

- They're as real as you, Averi.

Averi turned now and stared with disbelief.

- That is to say, they are as much a part of the dream as you. Why such incredulity? Was it not your discovery that everything is Consciousness? Waldo and Hap are equal in substance to all your other thoughts about yourself. Did you not discover that Averi himself is mere thought? But it is true; they do have a unique quality. And this is their gift – for you to discover why they emerged in the first place. You said quite specifically, if I remember rightly, that they don't so much as talk to you as talk to each other. Is that right?

- Yeah. But now I think about it they do kinda talk to me. Like Waldo will talk sometimes as if he's talking about Hap, or Hap about Waldo; but most often they talk to each other. Like I am Hap talking to Waldo; or I am Waldo talking to Hap.

- Can you give me an example of what they say?

Averi felt as if he were being squeezed of his most intimately personal secret. It was so terrifying he felt the inside of his stomach shake.

- Well, it's weird 'cos I don't generally remember afterwards. But recently Hap was telling Waldo that it was time to break down walls that he didn't even know were there.

The minute Averi said the words, he smiled.

- And do the words remain in your head?
- No. I speak them out loud.
- Anywhere?
- It could be. But I'm always alone, or out of earshot.
- Okay.
- And they come in different accents, too.
- Different accents?
- Uh huh.
- How wonderful! And is there a trigger for their arrival?
- No, but I can feel them when they're about to come.
- How do you mean?
- Well, there's kind of an atmosphere. Or like an inward pull into their energy. I don't know if that makes sense.
- Are they frightening?

Averi was surprised by the question.

- No, of course not. I like it when they come.

Nyx smiled.

- *What*, Averi asked. Is it less crazy if I *don't* like it?

Now she laughed.

- I wouldn't worry too much about 'crazy'. Tell me, have they come recently?

- Not so much while I've been with you. But, yeah, they come.

- Good.

- *Good?*

- Averi, can you not see the Grace in their appearance? They are an appearance in Consciousness to help you awaken to Self. Self is speaking to you via Waldo and Hap. They emerge for whatever lesson is required in a given moment. And just like Hap said, they have come to break down walls. They represent the conditioned mind and they represent the purified mind, both aspects. They have been tapping you ever so gently on the shoulder since childhood, reminding you that you are that which is prior to all experience. Can you not see that all your experiences once understood are your learning for remembering Self? Do not fight them or be ashamed of them. You don't have to share them with anyone else, if that's what you're worried about. And rest assured they will empty themselves back into Nothing as soon as they are no longer needed. What a carnival, what a compote of colour in this theatre! So many characters, so many themes, all leading to the one theme. And once again they are proof of the myriad ways in which Consciousness shall manifest to get our attention, be it a storm, a Nyx, a Waldo or a Hap.

Averi looked out at the mirror of slate and breathed the salty tang. He remembered the morning of the storm when seeing had so profoundly shifted within him. Now he realised that the hum he had discovered then – the hum of Existence – was the exact same hum which accompanied Waldo and Hap.

- You're right. They speak from Truth.

- Yes. They speak from Truth and as Truth; for they are Truth.

- Nyx?

- Yes, Averi.

Averi stood up, offered his arm and they started to walk again, taking careful, deliberate steps down the slope.

- The night before that first awakening to Self, when I was cooking in the kitchen and realised I was watching thought, I had a dream. It got to me all day. Patch had spoken to me in my dream. He had said, *I'm not sure you've given up life to be able to topple me yet.* I had no idea what he meant, but somehow, and I don't know why, it scared the hell out of me.

- And now?

They had reached the end of the slope and Nyx let go of Averi's arm. She crossed to the edge of the planks to where the L-shaped jetty began and sat with her legs dangling over the side.

- Well—

- *I'm not sure*, Nyx repeated, *you've given up life to be able to topple me yet.*

Averi sat down beside her. She was shaking her head, and if he was not mistaken, it looked as if her eyes were filling.

- Nyx?

Nyx turned to Averi and the full depth of her knowing shone as ebony.

- Can you not see the perfection of this one?

- This one?

- This *you*. How wisdom manifests and whispers Truth.

- How do you mean?

- Averi, what did we discover? That absolute wisdom is a surrendering of life to Life. All aspects of this personality must be cleared of their identifications. How much easier it is to lie than tell the truth. Even when we think we are speaking Truth, mind has crept in and taken ownership of a new spiritual identity. Even good intentions are lies. So what is required? A rigorous eye, that is all. So that every last drop of this person may be brought into your awareness and seen through the light of Compassion. Even poetics can trap us. Be wary of those, for they are subtle. The poet is God's orator, but how quickly the orator becomes enamoured with words, believing them to be his own; how quickly he is seduced by the beauty of their sounds, forgetting the hum from which they emanate. I say this only to prepare you for the subtle antics of this monkey mind, so that when he plays you may not take him so seriously. I say this because your own wisdom was warning against the mind's inevitable jump to want to evangelise and share its new wealth. Self came in the form of Patch as loving warning. The new spiritual mind shall be eager to topple all other minds, particularly those of our loved ones. But you remain the silent watcher even to this most urgent desire. If words are to come they shall find their voice effortlessly and with perfect timing.

Now that you are about to find your place again in the world you shall discover that others will notice much change in you. Some will accuse you of craziness. Yes, I know what a trigger this is for you. So, you must be on the lookout for your mind's reaction. It will be quick to build walls around itself in defence of intuitive knowing. But who is this one who feels in need of defence? Do you see the gift of such an accusation? It is a gift to bring you back to You. Many comments, many questions may come. You will know which questioners are earnest seekers of Truth, and if they ask and you find words flowing then you shall know those words to be pure. But avoid the temptation to tell them what they are not ready to hear, Averi. Remember that Life knows precisely what it is doing, and as you know, when Self calls out to Self, there is no choice but to hand oneself over.

Nyx turned now to the sea and to the seals that were playing in between the posts of the jetty. An adult was belly up and floating, while her pup was trying to hitch a ride. Averi watched as Nyx smiled and as the youngster, growing bored with his game, swam over to investigate them instead.

- Nyx?
- Uh huh?
- Is Self-recognition available to all?
- You mean—
- I mean like what about someone who's so lost in their story that they've created extra stories on top of their stories? Or like someone who's lost all mental capacity.
- Like your father?
- Sure, like my dad, but also like, well you know—
- Are you so different from those beings who create stories within their stories?

Averi swallowed hard.

- Are not Waldo and Hap exactly that? A delusion within the delusion? But if everything is Consciousness, how can there be concern? For some beings the accumulation of story is so strong, so dense, it is simply not possible to unpick themselves in one lifetime. Perhaps their role is another. Perhaps their delusion is someone else's awakening. There is a perfection to this timing, Averi. And remember that there is a bigger picture here. See how the mind limits itself to the destiny of one individual. We have seen there is no such thing as an autonomous individual. Each story fits into the greater story of the collective mind, which itself is the story within the Great Story of Consciousness. We have not yet dived into the intricacy of the collective mind. We can begin exploring this divine labyrinth in our next enquiry. For today, all you need to know is that each role has a profound part to play in this plot. Do not underestimate the beauty, the perfection that manifests as so-called imperfection. You remain as the silent principle, as that which is aware of the I Am that you Are, and then you tell me if Self-recognition is available to all.

Nyx smiled and slid her mittens under her legs.

Only the herring gulls were heard as if from some far distant land. Averi looked to the sea, his erstwhile companion, and squinted as the sun crept through. He understood and didn't understand, both at the same time.

- You know, Averi. I once knew a young girl who believed her head was purple.

Averi laughed through his nose.

- Her *head*?

- Yeah! Not the rest of her. Only her head. The minute she looked in the mirror all she saw was a great purple head and a normal-coloured body.

- Come on!

- I'm serious! This poor kid, she couldn't even go to school. She was convinced that everybody would be horrified by her head. More than that, she was convinced it was unlucky in some way, that it could cause harm to other people without her even trying. So they took her to doctors, who tried to tell her that it wasn't real. They pumped her with drugs to try and quell her anxiety and keep her quiet. No one thought to ask *why* she believed her head was purple. They just told her she was wrong. Years went by, no friends, no relationships, no lasting jobs, until she was so afraid, so repulsed by herself that she remained locked indoors. Until one day a young florist—

- A florist?

- Uh huh ... moved into town and heard of this strange purple-headed recluse. For some reason she was intrigued and so she put together a spray of ox-eye daisies and wild yarrow and paid the girl a visit. Now something told this wise florist that the girl was purple for very good reason, and would remain so until she faced whatever inner turmoil was needed to be faced. Obviously the girl sensed the compassion and over some time allowed the florist access into her world. Weeks, months went by as trust was slowly built. And then one day quite by chance the florist found a photograph tucked away in a book. She could see straight away from the resemblance that this was the girl's mother who had died giving birth to her daughter. The girl had come out of the womb with the cord wrapped around her neck and was understandably the deepest of all purples. Now, I don't need to tell you the rest. But suffice to say, once the girl had unwound herself of her anguish and guilt, she resumed with absolute radiance a normal-coloured head. And of course the next thing that happened was that she woke up to Self, saw everything as dream and lived the rest of this dream happily ever after.

Averi looked at Nyx sideways and then suddenly swore.

- Nyx!

- What? So, sure, I made it up, but I think my point was made, if not so subtle. When I say everything is Consciousness that includes purple heads and all heads and all the intricate workings within the relative head. What beauty there is in understanding this weave and how uniquely it spins out each of us. With some beings the personal weave is so tight, that this must first be loosened before they are ready to discover the Impersonal. Other beings have a different path. They must be whacked instead on the back of the head, have a trawler and a fifty-foot wave capsize them before they discover the Truth of what they are. Do you remember what I said to you on the beach that day? That you were being offered the most divine gift: to *die before you die*. Not such a crazy notion after all, huh? The most divine gift you as an individual can offer to other individuals is to look to your Self, to not turn your back on Love when it comes, to surrender this one who holds on so tenaciously to an idea of himself, and to discover your Real Nature. Divine Selfishness, we might call it, is the most loving, giving, compassionate expression available to us. Reside there and discover if it bears any resemblance to the selfishness of ego.

The seal pup was ducking and diving for attention, but as soon as its mother had signalled her catch, he was at her side in an instant. Nyx had turned to watch and her mouth dropped open in fascination.

- Nyx?
- Uh huh?
- Were you always like this?

She laughed and drew her knees to her chest.

- When did you get that tattoo on your back?

For the first time Averi saw Nyx genuinely startled. She opened her mouth as if to say, how on earth do you know I have a tattoo, but instead she could only laugh.

- I like it. But why that one in particular?

- Oh, you know, she replied. From the days when I took my name to heart.

She was looking straight at him now, twinkling those stars. Strands of her dark brown hair had caught in her mouth. Averi found himself pulling them free, and before there was time for thought to come in, she had reached across and kissed him on the lips. Now it was Averi's turn to be startled, and he laughed.

- What was that?

- I told you, Averi, that to be awake to the Truth of one's nature is not to be comatose on a spiritual pedestal. Experiencing is the way of this manifest existence. Don't forget that all feelings and emotions are available to you. They're a part of this great play. And what more beautiful expression of the Divine than the love experienced between two beings? The personal is experienced within the Impersonal; only then is the experience free.

Averi nodded and grinned.

- Are you saying you love me?

- I'm *saying*, she grinned, that I told you we would meet when you no longer needed me.

Averi laughed and held his face in his hands.

- What? The monkey mind is embarrassed now? You thought you were going to be a monk? Beauty manifests in so many ways, Averi. But as you have already seen, from the position of Self, there's no need left to hold on to it.

Her hair fluttered back and Averi pulled it aside once more. Desire arose, fresh and free. He leaned in and then froze. Across the water came a four-toned chorus.

- *Skipper!*

Both Nyx and Averi stood up to see them. Yellow bibs and braces, waders and aprons and the red woollen hat of a giant. A sting caught in Averi's throat. How they waved their arms with demented excitement: Trindar, Raul, Haiti and Patch, standing up from the deck of the *Chariot*, such welcome he could hardly bear.

Nyx slid her hand into his and waited.

Averi looked to Nyx and smiled at her patience.

- Now you're ready to face them, she said. Each one.

2

~**L**ili?

I have a feeling someone has been calling me for a while now. Gently and persistently.

- Lili, are you awake?

My goodness, my body has the weight of ten boulders.

- Look at you!

I manage to turn my shoulders to see Mareka standing in the doorway. She steps forward to take a closer look at me. With her hands clasped, her head bowed and her thin pointy nose, she shall remain forever my kind dormouse.

- You look like you slept the sleep of an angel, she says.

All I know is that my joints feel nailed to the bed.

- What time is it?

- Just gone eleven.

- What?

- I know, Mareka apologises, but I couldn't bear to wake you. Even Anastasia said to leave you.

- She *did*?

Mareka giggles as she nods. I haul myself up and Mareka rushes forward to push my pillow to support me. It feels like I have woken up into some alternate universe in which Anastasia is no longer the wicked queen, but my fairy godmother.

- Is she here?

- Yes, but she's on the war path. Someone managed to stuff all the plastic teaspoons down the drain in the sink.

Oh well, maybe not quite so alternate.

- Lili?

Mareka has turned to my desk and is picking up a piece of paper. There is a strange tone to her voice, as if she were trying not to cry.

- Doctor Wood left this earlier.

- What is it?

There *are* tears in Mareka's eyes, but her smile is full of joy.

I look to the paper and read my name. There are lots of typed notes and bureaucratic boxes. I'm not exactly sure what I am looking at. I look to Mareka and shake my head. She leans in and points her finger to one word.

'Discharged.'

I am so stunned my words are dry.

- Doctor Kolinsky faxed over her copy to Doctor Wood and Doctor Wood did the final sign-off this morning.

- While I was sleeping?

- Yes. While you were sleeping. You are free to go.

I stare up into Mareka's face. There is such warmth in those small grey lights that I am overwhelmed.

- Would you like me to help you pack?

I splutter as I laugh.

- Thank you. But I think I can manage.

There is so little that belongs to me in this room that I would be hard pushed to fill a handbag. Mareka acknowledges this with her apologetic smile.

- Well, I'll leave you to get ready.

- Does Reynardo know?

- Not yet. The art room was opened up this morning and everyone went down there after breakfast. Everyone except Greg.

- Does he know?

- No. He hasn't come out of his room yet. … Lili?

- Yes?

- I'm really happy for you. John, the night warden, told me how late you stayed with Doctor Kolinsky. Until almost ten. I've never known a doctor to be so dedicated. You must have had a lot to talk about. It's so clear that you cannot push a person to speak. But when they are ready all the words will come.

All I can do is nod, because if I talk I know I will cry.

- And now, Lili, you are free.

- Yes, Mareka, I am.

She stoops to kiss my cheek and then leaves me.

I look down at my discharge note still in my hands and wonder about those fingers that typed it. Did she go to her office straight away, or decide after a deep sleep of rest, waiting to be doubly sure? I shall never know. But this note alone tells me more than I could ever have imagined.

Suddenly the movement to be gone is strong. I push back the covers, throw off my pyjamas, and jump into the shower to wash off the antiseptic smell. Soaping happens, washing happens, drying happens, moisturising happens, brushing teeth happens, dressing happens, until I am standing in my worldly possessions. A pair of old Levis, a long-sleeved thermal, a burgundy jumper with one of those over-sized roll necks, my battered leather boots, and my black anorak. What I came in with and what I shall leave with. There is very little else to take. It fills a small plastic bag: jogging pants and a sweatshirt, my toothbrush and toothpaste, a hairbrush and – last of all – the glazed ceramic bowl from art class. My throat burns to see such love. You can see it is the work of a perfectionist – the red letters of Lili, the perfect strokes of an artist. I put it in the bag before I start to indulge.

It suddenly feels important to be gone before they get back for lunch. I reach the door and turn around. There is no sentiment, just gratitude for these four green walls. What lies are woven and fed in this place; but how humbling to see their part in this play.

I turn the handle, step into the hall, and stop. It is so pure I cannot move. Soft, precise and plucked, like a lament from a lost age. My feet walk me silently to Greg's door. There he is, perched on the end of his bed, his tufty head bowed over strings, his fingers running like silk. So exquisite, so innocent, such beauty that I don't know how the world is not forever weeping. It does not let me stay to watch. It pushes my legs and walks me away, out of this place. There is a rumpus to my right. Anastasia is squawking at Ashton, the cleaner, who is down on his knees with his head in the sink cupboard. Something about unblocking the pipe of spoons. Mareka is trying to make a suggestion, but is scolded. They do not see me. I barely hear them. I only hear the guitar. A consultant I don't know is walking towards me. He seems to know who I am and realises that I am leaving. He keys in the code to unlock the door and lets me out without even saying goodbye, too busy it seems with his own agenda. There is the lift in front of me. I take it to the ground floor, and step out in front of Carl at reception. I am reminded of our escapade with a bomb and a filing cabinet. It makes me smile. Perhaps he, too, is remembering, because he is smiling as I write my final signature. We exchange goodbyes without explanation and I walk to the glass double doors.

I zip up my anorak as I step outside. There is the bite of December and the crisp of frosted grass. The sky is white and empty. It feels like snow is coming. As I turn into the path I realise that the art room is only across the quad, in the old part of the building that juts out into the car park. There is a path intersection coming up. If I take the left-hand fork I shall not have to pass under the window. I am already close enough to see them from here. I can see Sarah raising her arms, no doubt exasperated at something; others just sit and stare or push paintbrushes, lethargically. The art therapist is helping someone with the pottery wheel. Rose is nose to paper, engaged in her world of colour groups; Lydia is sitting on her own, both elbows on the table, picking at her lip. My first pang comes. Who will look after this angel? It is as if he has heard my question, for Reynardo is suddenly face-to-the-window, and waving. He lifts up a new bowl he has crafted, obviously still wet. We stand there, the two of us, he inside, me on the path, and look to one another. The fox and his Lili. It feels for a moment unbearable to leave without saying goodbye. But the fox doesn't seem worried. He lifts his hand and waves, those wrinkles splitting like love. And then he turns and walks to the kiln.

I laugh and splutter my tears in one. What to say, but each day scours me clean. That broad haze of a winter sun is straining to get through. I have not a penny in my purse, nor an inkling of what will come. Somehow my legs are walking. What a wide crest at the rim of this jump. There's nothing to do but free-fall, and see where this One takes me.

Made in the USA
Middletown, DE
24 March 2021